TENNIS—One Shot at a Time

TENNIS—One Shot at a Time

Keep it Simple, Have More Fun

By
Ron Mescall
and
Chris de Brauw

All drawings by Ron Mescall

iUniverse, Inc.
New York Lincoln Shanghai

TENNIS—One Shot at a Time
Keep it Simple, Have More Fun

iUniverse, Inc.

For information address:
iUniverse, Inc.
2021 Pine Lake Road, Suite 100
Lincoln, NE 68512
www.iuniverse.com

ISBN: 0-595-32333-2

Printed in the United States of America

To Kim, Ronnie, Kara and Diane

Contents

Introduction ix

Preface: Visualizing the Game, One Shot at a Time xi

CHAPTER 1 Focus on Returning to the Game of Tennis 1

CHAPTER 2 Consistency Is An Attitude 4

CHAPTER 3 Practice, Practice 9

CHAPTER 4 Knowing why you play Tennis 14

CHAPTER 5 Tennis Intelligence 19

CHAPTER 6 Competition for Fun 27

1. Keeping the ball in play 29

2. Playing your game 30

3. Focus 31

4. Making small adjustments 33

5. Patience 36

CHAPTER 7 Strategy and Tactics 38

CHAPTER 8 Think Doubles Tactics for Fun 43

The "One up-one back" Formation 48

Serving Strategies 51

Other Tactics 53

Choosing Positions To Attack From 54

Mixed Doubles: The Fun Tactics of Give and Take 56

Ron's Golden Rules for Mixed Doubles 59

CHAPTER 9 The Amateur Tennis Tournament Experience 60

Chapter 10 Introducing Kids to Tennis 64
Court Games to Make Learning Fun 67
Chapter 11 The Role of the "Tennis Parent" 73
Chapter 12 Practical Tips 77
Basic Tennis Etiquette 77
Choosing a Tennis Racket 80
Re-stringing and Choosing String 83
Tennis Elbow 85
How to Play a Tie-Breaker 86
Ways to Set Up Recreational Tournaments 87
Chapter 13 Personal Stories 95
When the Garfield Tennis Courts were Clay (Ron's Story) 95
How I Found Out About Yoga (Chris' story) 96

Introduction

This book offers a simple approach to having fun at the game of recreational tennis. In these pages we share some of our ideas and mental tips to show you the way to really enjoy the game of tennis.

Tennis is a competitive sport, certainly, but for most of us it should mostly be devoted to having fun, as well as providing fun and pleasure for all others involved.

In other words, this book is for those of us who look at tennis as a form of recreation and exercise.

We think of tennis as a game of shot making, one shot at a time. The fun of tennis is, in our minds, feeling the power of the shot. We have pulled together some basic ideas and tips that help us to experience the thrill of solid, powerful shot making:

- Simplicity
- Commitment and effort
- Focus
- Creativity and spontaneity
- Discovering a positive mindset
- Winning for fun, but never at all cost
- Finding people you enjoy playing and competing with
- Making tennis a fun game for kids

The different chapters in the book address different ideas. While the entire book is meant as an easy read, some chapters may be more to the point for you than others. So, pick and choose.

For simplicity, the book is written in the masculine, but it is, of course, meant as much for female readers and tennis enthusiasts as their male counterparts.

Ron Mescall Sr. grew up in Indianapolis, Indiana. He won Junior Titles twice and played on the Central Indiana Junior Davis Cup team. He continued playing as a scholarship player at Michigan State University, winning the No. 5 Singles Big Ten Championship. He has been a high school coach and teacher, and tennis professional for 40 years. He received his BA and MA while at State in Education.

As the resident tennis professional at the Eagle Ridge Inn and the Galena Territory, in Galena Illinois, Ron has written countless (tennis) advice columns for the "Territory Times", a weekly publication for the residents of the Galena Territory. And, Ron is a regularly published cartoonist.

Chris de Brauw is a devoted tennis enthusiast. Born in The Netherlands, he grew up playing such esoteric (for the US) sports as cricket and field hockey, and didn't begin taking his tennis game serious until he moved to the US in 1971. As a long-time resident of the Galena Territory, he and Ron play tennis for fun on many a weekend. His other hobbies include yoga and playing the flute.

Chris is a market research consultant in Chicago, Illinois. He has a BA from the University of Amsterdam in Political Science, and an MA in Communications from Ohio University.

The authors would like to thank Heidi Sauser and Donna Thompson-Brent for their generous help in preparing this manuscript.

Preface: Visualizing the Game, One Shot at a Time

Think of the tennis shot as an adventure. Visualize each shot as you pick up the image of the ball, and play your game one shot at a time. Creative play is simple when you move from shot to shot while staying as much as you can "in the moment".

Keep your tennis simple. Let your spirit for the shot carry you from point to point.

Begin every stroke with determination and try hard to be efficient. With every movement you encourage yourself to use your imagination to come up with a return, and the chance for winning the point.

How we play the tennis shot may turn out to be more important than we imagine, for it signifies nothing less than our being in the world. Create a mood that encourages spontaneity and focused participation. There should be a joyous and humorous interaction in your mind as you formulate the vision of the shot.

Put yourself in a frame of mind where you may learn simply by playing the shot hard and fair. Try to realize the best shot you have ever hit in that situation. Every shot has a purpose. Value the quality of each movement in the shot and remain mentally flexible.

Don't chase your focus away with too much competitiveness. Reject the outside influences, stay focused and drive yourself from point to point. Outside images can destroy the shot even if you have created sound fundamentals. Don't think about the previous point, or your last shot, only be with the shot you are playing right now.

Your thoughts carry you from point to point. Realize your dreams in the shot. Visualize it as a pleasant struggle you come to terms with. And always remember that, if you have reached too high or tried to do too much, there is the chance to win the next point.

The shot becomes a group of feelings in this mental game. Enjoy the struggle for happiness and excitement. Perhaps, picturing the best shot in this situation is what we call "focus" and concentration. Put it all together in one great surge to the ball and create a powerful challenge to your opponent's game.

Establish a realistic goal for improvement with a mental picture of yourself. Discover the success mechanisms within you. You must break old mental habits by taking a "new look" at yourself—changing your perspective from negative to positive. It's so ironic that the shot, how we approach it, is like our own life and successes.

We have pulled together a set of ideas to form your own road map towards a simple and exciting tennis game plan. Your game plan becomes an inner drive towards solid, creative, exciting stroke production. Learn to attack and deploy your strengths in each shot against your opponent. Our final thought in each shot is to make it, create the chance to win, *and to have fun while doing it.*

We must play with intensity, discipline, concentration and determination. The goal is to develop a sense of pride in our ability to play tennis with imagination and vision, while maintaining sound fundamentals and consistency.

No one sport obviously will fulfill the needs and drives for every person. But tennis has many unique and desirable qualities, which indicates that it deserves a large role as a recreational sport for all ages.

1

Focus on Returning to the Game of Tennis

Everyone is looking for ideas for new and more satisfying ways to live. The game of tennis is a great way to express that desire, so come and have an adventure with others that are interested.

There are so many aspects of our potential that we can develop:

Having fun in tennis can be free and foolish, liberating and satisfying, so let your spirit carry you to any level of the game you feel comfortable with.

Each individual can attain a realistic self-image of strengths and deficiencies. Enjoy the good life with tennis as part of an energetic lifestyle. Make the most of every minute and put off the time of physical inactivity, which is causing so much degeneration and obesity in our society.

Develop within yourself and with everyone around you a drive and desire for personal physical activity. Recognize in tennis your ideal self-image. Relax and assess yourself. Establish realistic goals for improvement that you can build on to further enhance the mental aspects of your game.

The most important game is "The Game of Life" and physical activity equals one of the major keys to personal success and well-being.

Come back to tennis and embark on a training program and give emphasis to that special training device called EFFORT.

Tennis can teach you how to endure and survive a crisis and how to meet it head-on. The main lesson in tennis is like the main lesson in life. That is, you never give up the fight, you keep trying, no matter how dismal the outlook.

Certainly, I have put a lot of time in tennis and worked hard as a youngster on my basic skills. I set certain goals and found great satisfaction as winning has become less important than when in college as an athlete. I still use tennis to improve my life and work on my weaknesses, both mentally and physically. Always remember its not too late to return to the game.

One of the greatest secrets of outstanding peak performance in tennis is learning to focus. Your best play occurs when you're thinking about the here and now. Thinking about the past will only bring on anger, regret and frustration. Control your concentration. Playing from point to point. Use deep breathing as a catalyst to free up your mind. Evolve your game plan, capitalizing on your strengths and exploiting the weaknesses of your opponent.

Before any match, create the feeling you want to invoke to get your most ideal performance state. This also works on the job and in teaching and coaching. Find

15 to 20 minutes of music that stimulates your feeling of confidence, enjoyment, focus and drive. Visualize your best shots and most outstanding performance state. It is a great experiment and music can aid individual thought and performance.

Tennis is a mental game. Always set positive goals. Bring focus and commitment to your playing and practice. Always know you can do it and think positively. Convert negative thoughts into positive thoughts. Think of your best shots as your stroke. Be flexible and adjust to change—be optimistic, enthusiastic and create intensity in the right direction.

2

Consistency Is An Attitude

The worst tactical error you can make in tennis is not keeping the ball in play. Consistency is the key to scoring points and one of the most important fundamentals of the game. You should always work toward improving "Stroke Production" and hitting your best shots at all times.

Hitting your best shot does not necessarily mean how hard you hit, or hitting a winner. In fact, your best shot should be the best you can produce given what your opponent sends your way.

- First of all, you must make sure to hit the ball back, across the net and in.
- Next, you will want to concern yourself about placement, the direction of your shot and how deep you send it into the court. Usually, hitting your returns with a good margin of safety (clearing the net by at least 2-3 feet) allows the ball to land deep in your opponent's side of the court.
- Lastly, you should think of spin and power. So only after you are sure you can get it back and feel where you are placing the ball should you concern yourself with how hard to hit the ball.

Attempting to hit your best shot will improve your strokes. It's like "Shot Selection" in basketball. You decide on the best course of attack each time you return the ball. Every shot must have a purpose.

Everyone should practice consistency. When practicing, think about getting the ball back every time. Always try to hit the ball on the first bounce, because that is what the game is all about. And it will improve your workout, raising your ability to react as well as your physical condition.

The three basic elements in "Stroke Production" are:

- Preparation,
- Hitting zone control and
- The finish and follow through tracking the ball.

Basically, be ready and have your racket back. Watch the ball hit your racket. Relax and keep breathing. Now watch your opponent's return. Know before his ball crosses the net whether you are going to take the ball on your forehand or backhand. This allows you to get ready for your next shot. Every time you hit, think about improvement, giving your best shot.

Use your court time to practice efficiently and effectively. Structure your practice on the idea of getting the ball back every time. Consistency is attitude, and on the tennis court it is at least as important as technique. Develop a positive attitude about "Consistency" and arrange everything you do in practice about this as a goal.

Turn this attitude into action as you play the game of tennis. We must realize early that the greatest impact on consistency is "attitude".

We must practice mental concentration to reach the level of consistency we want.

Improve your chances for success by focusing your complete attention on looking at the ball. Neither the eye nor the mind should be bothered by outside pressures.

Prepare early for the shot. Early preparation is an important factor in your concentration.

Hitting against a board or flat surface establishes repetition that leads to building your mental and physical confidence.

Give yourself positive reinforcement as you take pride in returning every shot. Your own positive reinforcement becomes the source of consistency.

When you reduce your anxiety, your mental and physical tensions lessen. Mental readiness is developed through proper execution.

You still need to think of the game as a fun activity. Avoid thinking of it as a burden or something threatening. You can raise your sense of security if you focus your feelings on the fact that we are playing for pleasure. It is not a great catastrophe to lose a point or game here and there. The game of tennis is very forgiving; you get lots of chances to make up for lost points and games.

Some of the smallest things you may do in practice could lead to great results. Always be honest with yourself and do things that you like. Prove yourself everyday as you work toward improved consistency.
(On the other hand, hitting a ball way out or over the fence, once in a while, can help you lift the seriousness of executing every shot, and create a relaxed readiness for productivity).

Communicate within yourself and strive for the best: Give total effort with total preparation.

Keep a strong relationship between fun and consistency. Have a winning attitude because you know you can get the ball back every time.

Don't let yourself be mentally fatigued. Train your mind to resist distraction. You can revise your basic look at the ball by tracking the seam or the underside of the ball. (For practice, try to improve your eyesight by reading road signs and billboards, and reading the numbers on license plates).

Always practice your concentration. Watch the ball hit your racket. Think about the shot you are making. Play knowing your ability to hit the best shot you have at the right time.

Remember to bounce, jump, hop and run full speed after the ball. Move forward for the ball rather than reaching for it. Have balance, which comes from getting ready and starting correctly and finishing with a great stroke. This also leads to concentration.

Increasing your confidence is the golden asset that will raise your entire game. You're not out there in the sun to experience exhilaration on every shot or execute beautiful shots each time, but you are there to be consistent as many times as possible.

Use your sense of imagination towards creating your best shot. Don't let your mind wander, because this will lead to your not completing your best shot.

Attacking smartly and probing with many of your shots will help your game. Get psyched for that shot and refer to your memory to make sure it's the best out of your mind-file for that placement. You'd better be ready to be consistent. Be internally motivated to execute your shots.

As a consistent player you have a role to play and you must identify it early. Take a relaxed point of view with one of your most important goals being to have "fun".

Promote success and deal with every situation. React to your own experiences and do your research as you identify the shortcomings in your stroke.

Develop a certain quantitative understanding of the geometric aspects of where it is easier to place the ball, which is usually back-to-where-it-came-from.

Meet the challenge according to your past experiences associated with consistency. Use your own incentives to reach these goals. Pick a shot and analyze how you best hit that shot in your mind.

3

Practice, Practice

Tennis is an action-packed sport that is tremendously challenging to a person's mental and physical abilities, and a healthy interest for both young and old.

It is a game for the entire family to enjoy and have fun with. It is a game of great carry-over value and can be played throughout life for physical fitness. But perfect style, experienced instruction and inexhaustible stamina and even the best strokes are no substitute for practice.

Practice will help develop the ability to respond automatically and make your actions into habits. You learn to create situations in practice and think under pressure.

Virtually everyone who plays tennis wants to improve stroke production, but the question is how to do it most efficiently and effectively.

Practices should be structured in a manner that allows players to hit a large number of balls in a short period of time.

Few players know how to organize a practice session. The best way to start is to set aside a specific period of time devoted to practicing with a partner of similar ability.

A common rule in tennis is: Play matches with better players, but practice with someone on your level and work on your weaknesses.

Focus on proper stroke production, and allow yourself to groove your shots. Along with the practice sessions it is also a good idea to set time aside for practicing court movement and physical conditioning.

Always start by making sure you keep the ball in play. Hit balls at a medium pace in a pressure-free environment. Don't keep score or keep comparing your strokes with your partner. Concentrate all your senses to the shot facing you and you will find real benefit from hitting with consistency.

Set a specific goal for each practice session. If you are an inexperienced player you need to devote more practice time to technique drills rather than match play drills. Work on your weaknesses, but also polish your strengths because they may be the key to your offensive attack. One of the most important factors in practice is to always hit the ball on the first bounce.

General technique drills should be a part of every player's practice session.

Drills can be structured to simulate "emergencies". For example, if a player hits consistently to your backhand (your weakest shot perhaps) this is one kind of an emergency. How often you respond to all these emergencies determines whether you win or lose. Prepare yourself to learn to react to the emergency situations.

If you are able to hit a shot down-the-line, for example, past and out of reach of the net man, an important factor that will determine whether you make the shot or not is how often you have drilled on that particular shot.

Do not stay on any drill too long. Remember the drills you like so you can continue them at another time.

If you seem to lose intensity in a drill, always remember to give emphasis again to playing every ball on the first bounce. Keep several balls in your pocket to keep play continuous if you make a mistake.

There is no limit to the number and variety of drills you can design. When you develop a drill, start with a goal and design the drill around that goal. Make drills fit your own special needs.

Decide what aspect of the game you would like to work on using your own creativity. Create mini-situations, which will help your strategy. Change drills you already know and make drills very simple.

Keep your play at a pace of intensity you can effectively be consistent.

There is no limit to the possibilities and playing specific points. Hit balls directly to your partner part of the time and vary your intensity.

Tennis is an intellectual game maintaining a continuous application of power, speed, and endurance. Gear your practice to cover all court areas and each part of your attack: The serve, the return, ground strokes, volleys, lobs and overheads.

Practice should be based on efficient learning, economy of time and the formation of habits that will benefit the simplicity of your game. Having to think less about it makes tennis more fun, and creates the confidence to compete. The desire for simplicity becomes a key factor in your overall philosophy.

Simplicity is the major factor in the process of improvement. Simplicity makes it easier to concentrate, and as your ability to concentrate grows, so will your game.

Always stretch and warm up before practice mentally as well as physically.

Here are thoughts, ideas and steps to consider when practicing:

1. Warm-up short court, (stand at the service line or just inside the service line)

2. Hit ball all on first bounce (always)

3. Play all balls in practice even if they are out. They build consistency and stamina, and help you stay intense during game "emergencies".

4. Watch the ball hit your racket strings. It leads to better concentration.

5. Learn to play on both sides when it's windy. Use the advantage of hitting harder when playing against the wind.

6. With the wind behind you, hit the ball on rise. Practice it.

7. Use a lower toss when serving in the wind. It helps your control. Practice it.

8. Move into every ball, don't let the ball play you.
9. Always hit for placement as you are developing consistency.
10. Have your racket back before you move to the ball.
11. Start rallies with a serve whenever you and your partner are near the baseline.
12. Aim well inside the lines, especially when hitting down the line
13. Get into a ready position, move your feet and keep making small adjustments to your position until you hit the ball.
14. Be flexible and bend your knees when hitting.
15. Track the ball with your eyes.
16. Exchange ideas with your partner in practice
17. Keep the ball in play at all costs.
18. Mix up serves and volleys along with return of service
19. Make up some game situations in practice
20. Practice footwork movement and racket control
21. Try adding some new shots to your offensive attack.
22. Use positive-reinforcement with your practice partner
23. Realize in practice you develop total effort with total preparation

Drills used in practice have an influence on your mental preparedness. We develop this motivation in practice and learn to play point to point.

Create a frame of mind built on simplicity and effort. Ultimately, mental fitness becomes just as important as the physical aspects of the game.

4

Knowing why you play Tennis

One aspect that can contribute to your enjoyment of tennis is having a better understanding why you play, what motivates you the most, and to seek out others who have similar reasons for playing.

The traditional way in which most tennis players are matched is by their rating. A tennis professional can give you a USTA rating, which is a number with one decimal point anywhere from 1.5–7.0, where 1.5 is a total beginner, a 5.0 is a very skilled club player, and 7.0 is a world class professional player. Most amateur players are rated somewhere between 2.5 and 4.5. (For a complete description of the USTA rating system visit the website www.usta.com and click on USA League Tennis, and then NRTP).

Someone who has about the same skill level as you may be a perfect person to play and compete with. But not always. If you and the other person play tennis for very different reasons, the time you spend with that other person on the court may not be as enjoyable, as when you play with people who share the same goals.

From spending many years on the courts, we have come to the view that there appear to be four basic motivations, or reasons, why people engage in sports and physical activities:

- Getting a good workout
- Winning
- Playing well, or trying to improve one's game
- Socializing

The interesting thing is that different people have different priorities when they go out and play.

For some, being with friends (Socializing), is the most important reason to play. That doesn't mean that other reasons, such as improving one's game, or winning, are totally unimportant. It's just that, in the end, the time spent together with friends is the most dominant reason for playing at all.

Others, for example, are especially competitive in nature. They love the fact that they are getting a good workout, and even that the fun of winning relates to playing against someone worthwhile to beat, but the best part of the game, after all, is the satisfaction of winning.

Professional athletes often are extremely competitive, as are most very advanced and successful athletes. The point is, many amateur players who love to play tennis are not that competitive in their outlook. When some people in a group are much more competitive than others, or when one person on a tennis doubles team is much more competitive than his or her partner, there's a chance that the outing is not as enjoyable or satisfying as when there's more agreement on this point.

There is also a subtle contrast between people who are really trying to play their best tennis ("Playing Well" dominates) compared to people who are primarily out for the exercise. To the latter, there's plenty of satisfaction in simply getting a workout. They accept that one day they play better than the next, and it doesn't bother them too much, because, after all, their most important reason for playing is the exercise, to get that pleasant feeling from a physical challenge and being all tired out in the end.

On the other hand, people for whom Playing Well dominates over the need to exercise are just that much more involved with tennis. These people may, in fact, engage in other activities to be in shape in order to play tennis. Their tennis does, of course, give them a good workout, but that is not their main goal. Playing tennis as well as possible is what involves them the most.

The sketch below shows how the four different motivations can be portrayed in relation to each other. Note that the horizontal axis describes how a player thinks about himself/herself, and that the vertical axis is an indication how a player relates to his fellow players or opponents. The opposing arrows are not really "opposites", but reflections of what is more important to you. It simply asks: When you play, what matters more, winning or being with your friends? And, what matters more to you, getting a good workout or playing well?

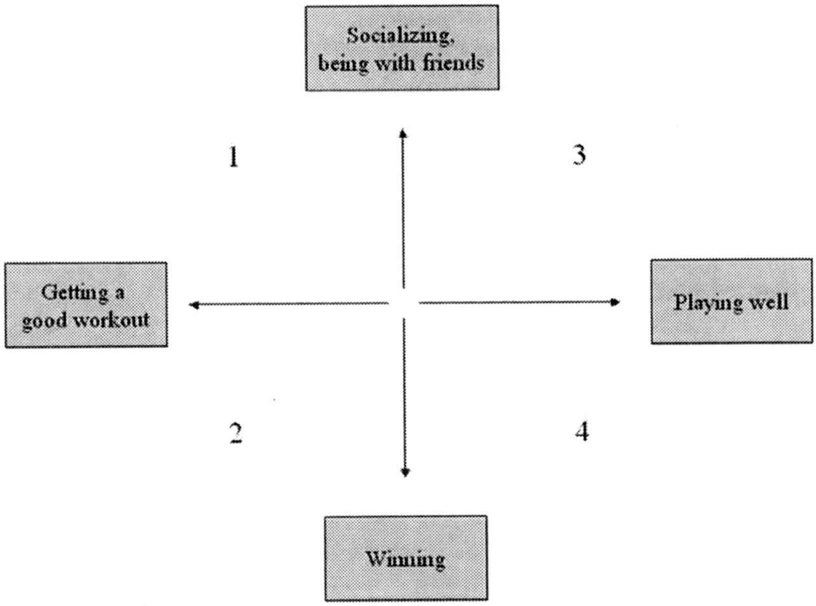

It now becomes possible to think of yourself, and other tennis players you know, in terms of which combination of motivations are most prevalent when playing, and to map where a person is likely to be on the grid.

1. People who play tennis primarily to be together with friends and to get some exercise would fall in sector #1. These are, most likely, the people who are not particularly ambitious about their tennis game. This may be a regular group of friends who love to get together for a weekly game of tennis. If it wasn't tennis, they might be playing cards. It just so happens that tennis gets

them outdoors, and some exercise, and that's what they enjoy about the activity, besides being with their friends.

This set of motivations might also occur among people who only play occasionally, or on vacation. A nice thing to do on a sunny day.

2. The players who are in sector #2 take their tennis more seriously, simply because they are competitive in nature. Tennis is one of the main ways, or the only way, they get physical exercise. When they get out on the court, it is for the exercise, but, to them, with exercise comes the fun of trying to win, trying to beat the person or team across the net. They are no tennis perfectionists. They work hard at keeping the ball in play, trying to beat their opponents in whatever way it takes. The thrill is in making the points.

   This is the weekend warrior class. In retirement communities you can see four guys over 60, or over 70, do whatever it takes to beat the other guys. When the game's over, everyone is friendly, but while the game is on, it can be tense. Winning matters more than how it is accomplished.

3. The players in section #3 take their tennis game more serious again. They are involved in the beauty of tennis. They want to hit good strokes, and when competing, move well, and select the right shot for the right situation. They love thinking about strategies. They love to watch tennis on TV, and may have a collection of tennis books. To them, it's a beautiful sport.

   At the same time, they may not be that competitive. For these people, playing a good point is more important than winning. They are not as hell-bent on winning as the players in sector # 2, simply because they are more into the process of playing than into winning. They express their desire to play better by taking tennis lessons and clinics.

   These people may have only limited experience with playing competitively in tournaments or tennis leagues. Rather, they maintain relationships with other players who feel the same way about tennis, that it's a great way to spend time with friends, and that, in the end, winning or losing is less important than trying to play up to your potential.

4. The players in sector #4 are the most advanced tennis players. For them, tennis is much more than social fun, it is something they are very good at. To a degree, tennis defines who they are. They have experience in competing, from league play, club tournaments, high school or college competition.

They spend a lot of time on getting better, for example, by training with a coach.

The ultimate satisfaction, for these players, is being able to win matches with their tennis skills, with their stroke making and their mental control, as well as with their competitive instincts.

At this point you may be thinking about yourself, which sector on the grid is most like you. You may, of course, be a "borderline case", not sure which side is more dominant, your interest in exercise or your interest in playing well. It may even depend on the circumstances, where you are and with whom. It may be a subtle distinction, but for most people, one of the two motivations (that do not seem to be "opposites") is stronger, more of what drives them to play.

You also may see why it is so much more fun to play with some people, and so much more frustrating with others. When play is frustrating, it is probably because the other person has such different goals than you. Don't quit playing tennis over that. It is worth your while to find people who have similar motivations for playing.

True, tennis is a game of skill, and, in order to have a competitive outing or match, it is best to find opponents who have about the same "rating as you do". But in the long run, you will get the most satisfaction out of your tennis when you find other players who approach the game of tennis with goals similar to yours.

"WATCH THE GOOD PLAYERS"

5

Tennis Intelligence

Your tennis skills will improve as you focus and correct your frame of mind. To improve your mental game, you need to learn to think positively and to suppress negative self-defeatist thoughts.

The intelligent approach to all learned skills focuses on these goals:

- Success—achievement, accomplishment
- Activity—emphasis on participation
- Approval—recognition, worth, attention
- Belonging—being wanted, group status
- Excitement—adventure, fun
- Creativity—new experiences, variety
- Cognition—learning and thinking

The fulfillment of these goals in tennis will influence everything connected with your game.

Eliminate failure experiences. Success leads to more success. Interim goals that are attainable are a very good beginning. Practice your basic motor skills.

Practice as you expect to play in competition—simple but sound. Let your personality have an impact on your play. Keep a deep emotional involvement. Be ready to focus your anger to stimulate your play. Don't let negative thoughts undermine your morale and increase your fatigue.

Use your sense of humor to relieve tension and be happy with small successes and build on them. Create positive results.

Observe your opponent and evaluate him intelligently. Use what you have determined during your warm-up about his level of playing ability. Observe your opponent during the match and capitalize on his weaknesses that emerge. The difference between winning and losing may be using your intelligence at any time.

Next, adjust your attack. For example, try hitting 90 percent of your first serves in.

Be a practical thinking player. Combine steadiness with forcing shots. Try to systematically break down your opponent's game with many individual forms of attack.
Keep your opponent off-balance by out-thinking him. Give him difficult shots to handle.

Control your thoughts and emotions, always working to master concentration excluding all outside stimuli. Work on your anticipation, intensity with enthusiasm and great effort. Believe in yourself.

We can only conclude that this is using your intelligence to its maximum. If you make an error, show your intelligence by not doing exactly the same thing again. The single-most important characteristic is concentration. Be flexible, but remain constantly alert, analyzing your own and your opponent's game.

Create an eagerness to do the correct thing and be like a lawyer handling each situation tactfully both in your mind and with your athletic competitiveness. Find alternative pathways to winning and getting satisfaction. Follow your game plan as it develops through your experience early in the match. Out-think your opponent.

Promote a "conditioned reflex" to some of the things you emphasize in your attack. Give yourself a pat on the back for a good shot, with a "yes", "great" or "excellent". Encourage your own success in your mind. This is an intelligent approach to self-esteem.

Imagination is a very important tool in your quest towards exploiting the weaknesses of your opponent. Be as positive as possible and learn to tolerate frustrations. Hold back impulses to react negatively towards yourself until a later time. Use your mind and intelligence to keep out anger. Keep thinking through the match, analyzing everything that you plan as you attack and attack.

Go to each point methodically leaving all bad activity in the past and move on.

Sometimes, rituals help control anxieties. For instance, you often see tennis players adjust their strings between points. This is a good ritual. Bouncing the ball a number of times before serving. Touching the net or touching the back fence between points is a ritual.

Choosing the right shot.

Correct tactics simply means being in the right place at the right time, and making the right shot at the right time.

Many tennis players have difficulty selecting the correct shot and sound tactics consistent with their own strengths and weaknesses. It means, during the warm-up, you must probe and analyze the weaknesses of your opponent.

Players who do not have super quick reactions, a strong serve and other special skills for successful net play, must go to the route of steady, accurate and consistent ground strokes. This is a very sound strategy and tactic to win: Get the ball back and let your opponent make the mistakes. Forcing your opponent into errors is a goal you must work towards as your game plan develops.

Anticipation is developed through experience, but you always have to be alert to the movements and position of your opponent. Certainly, you can arrive at the right position to hit if you have your racket back before getting to position—a factor that may improve your consistency by 30-40 percent!

Tennis is a high level mental game. True tactics of hitting the right shot are based on thinking.

Remember that many believe the serve is the biggest single weapon in tennis ("the opening gun"). But if you only have a fair serve—placement and depth are an extremely important factor. You have the power to choose where to hit the ball.

Through experience you of course learn to correct the right time to employ your skills into the correct shot. Always, as we have mentioned earlier, think of hitting the best shot you have when faced with this situation, whether it be a passing shot or a lob.

There are several classes of shots in your skilled game plan:

- Using a defensive type shot
- A smashing attack shot
- Keeping the ball in play
- Moving your opponent
- Setting your opponent up
- Keeping the ball down the middle
- Drop shot, bringing your opponent close to the net
- Angle shot to keep your opponent off balance.

All of the above require footwork and position. They also require the important factor of anticipation. By combining defensive and aggressive play, along with sound principles of position, you can succeed in long rallies waiting for the right time to select the correct shot and attack to make the kill.

Make your opponent play badly. The steady player can throw off the big hitter when everything comes back. Use sound baseline steadiness, accuracy, depth and employ a great game plan in your mind based on craftiness. This is how I (Ron) won a Big Ten Championship in the early 60's.
Few outstanding game plans can leave out the volley and aggressive net game. But first you must set your opponent up.

Most of the modern day books on tennis are based on skills exemplified by the great modern professional players. Unfortunately, we who play after work or on the weekend fall into a more recreational classification. We must use a game plan based on our thought and mind experience. We cannot rely on powerful serve and volley all the time. Sometimes we just hope the ball gets over the net.

However, it is always important that we strive for improving our skills and increase our game as we learn through great experiences playing with our friends and, maybe, being in a tournament once-in-a-while. Who is to say we do not get just as much out of tennis as the pro's? Many times we wander between the fantasy of being a great player and reality, as we sit down on the park bench.

We are born with certain abilities, but we must create our skill. Excellent tennis is a display of skill based on thinking. It is based on years of concentrated effort and discipline. Be steady, hit deep and wait for the right shot to put away.

Choosing the correct shot out of our game plan is an accomplishment in and of itself. And, it can be enough to tip the scales in your favor. For example, making a good deep placement, followed by an angled volley. This could be a particular game change for you if you have been riding the baseline all through the match. But if you are on the losing end, consider selecting other shots in your skills frame of reference.

In my years of coaching college and high school players, I have often seen that players like to practice and look good using their *best* shots. The answer is to practice the skills you *do not do well*, and to create point and game situations that call for the skills you have trouble with.

Don't underestimate your ability to improve your choice of shots as you play. Most of the time we are just scratching the surface of our brain and through focusing we can drive ourselves into situations, and experience successes we never imaged we had.

Many times, as a youngster, I have sat down on the park bench at the courts in Garfield Park in Indianapolis and played matches in my mind. Certainly, it was dreaming, but it is something I would encourage in any particular sport or even business you are involved in. Dreaming is an important part of life.

As a teacher, having taught for over 37 years, I have encouraged students to look outside the window in health class when I taught on the top floor of Jefferson Junior High in Dubuque, Iowa. I have encouraged students to dream so that they could at some time think through goals that might influence success in their life. What can you imagine out there, getting away from reality that holds a new experience; a dream that will form an interim goal for improving your situation in life?

Often times I think this is a factor to improve self-esteem, although I always encouraged students to do something nice for another as a bridge to improving their own self esteem. Several times I began class with "what have you done for someone else today".

This all relates to choosing the right tennis shot because until you learn to dream you will be chasing success but never catch up.

Play your own game based on sound thinking but if you get to a point where you decide you can not go any further, sit down on the bench at the park with no one around and open other doors of your brain by dreaming.

Sound tactics means knowing your own strengths and weaknesses. Excellent tennis is not just power and hard hitting, but, rather, simplicity gained through years of practice and discipline. Many pro's indicate it takes 5 years to become a player. Perhaps that's the reason tennis is on the decline. Kids do not want to devote the time, where in other cases kicking the ball comes easier to most.
You must feel a drive to improve skills and give the time to the game.

Having a certain style of play is valuable, and choosing the right shot to go on offense or defense, or simply to prolong the point, is an art. A player may attack on defense as well as offense. He may vary his play with a mix of topspin, lobs, short shots and depth. All must be done with the drive and consistency of an artist, putting total intention into the shot (one shot at a time!), executing the overall game plan by choosing the "right shot" as much of the time as possible.

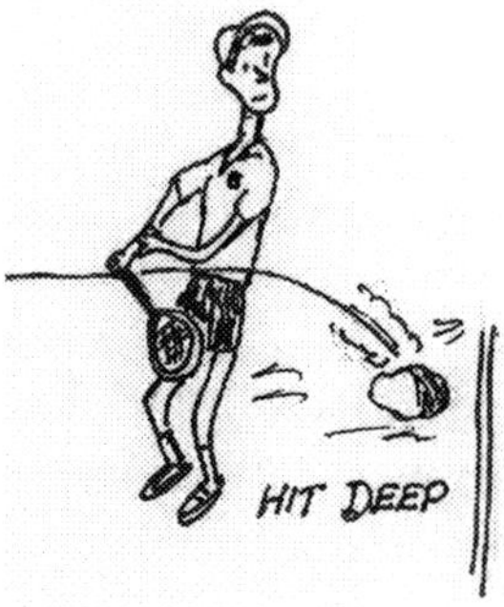

6

Competition for Fun

You're watching an exciting tennis match on television. Probably it's an advanced round in a professional tournament, like one of the Master's Series, or a Grand Slam, like Wimbledon or the US Open. For a long time, there's no way to tell who is going to win, but in the end, one of the players pulls off the victory. It was a thriller, lots of fun to watch. Those players competed like their lives depended on it...

Immediately, the players' emotions are shown in great detail. The winner is beaming, with arms raised, basking in the applause, waving at the crowds, blowing a kiss to the friend's box, where coaches, relatives and the girlfriend are hugging each other. The loser sits down, packs his gear, looks dejected. Soon he walks off the court lugging a bag full of rackets as large as a small footlocker....

In the pro game, and among the super-serious tennis players who play tournaments for a district or national tournament ranking, the euphoria about a victory and the disappointment about losing are understandable. But, for the recreational player, winning or losing shouldn't be that important. There is no more glory in winning your match from your regular tennis buddy than the satisfaction that, today, what you tried to do, worked. The fun was in trying to win, not to "defeat" your friend. For the loser, there is no point in getting too upset about losing, if you gave it your best effort. You got a great workout; you probably won almost as many points as your opponent, just not the ones that decided the final outcome.

The whole idea of competing for fun is that recreational tennis is more interesting and enjoyable when each side really tries to win. The idea is simply that each player does his best to give the person on the other side of the net a challenge to overcome. Basically, if you go out on the court with the desire to try to do your best, your share of wins will happen, regardless when they occur. But best of all, you give yourself and your opponent a good time.

Anger ruins it for everyone

We have all been around the recreational player who is so intent on winning that, the moment things don't go right, he gets down on himself, starts berating himself for "stupid" errors, and before you know it, he is throwing or bouncing his racket and the cursing begins. Soon, he is making more and more errors, because he is trying to make up for falling behind with riskier shots. Worse still, sometimes he even needs to express his anger (at himself) with furious serves, which, of course, mostly go into the net or way out.

This person has lost the idea of competing for fun. Not only is he ruining the game for himself, but for everyone else on the court as well. Instead of trying to give the other person his best effort, he is undermining the whole idea of giving each other a challenge. He is making himself the challenge. Really, when you think about it, it's kind of selfish to lose your cool in a recreational game of tennis.

The most famous tennis player who knew how to use anger to his own advantage is John McEnroe. His outbursts, usually directed at referees, were legendary. Often, he was able to channel his anger into raising his game. At the same time, he often managed to disrupt his opponent's level of concentration. Importantly, he directed his anger at others more so than at himself. His behavior was tolerated at best, and taken for what it was: An expression of his extreme competitiveness on the pro circuit. In fact, when you see him compete today in the Seniors Circle, you can still see his competitive fire.

Typical recreational players, who play 1-3 times a week at best, usually cannot channel their anger into better play. There is far too much of a risk that anger will distract you from your game. It disrupts your concentration, especially if you focus your anger at yourself.

Just remember, the idea is to create a challenge for your opponent. Then you'll have fun.

The basic steps involved in competing for fun and creating a challenge for your opponents are:

1. Keeping the ball in play
2. Playing your game
3. Focus
4. Making small adjustments
5. Patience

1. Keeping the ball in play

This idea is so fundamental that people often forget that it, more than anything else, is what makes tennis fun. Nothing is more exhilarating than playing a prolonged point where the ball keeps going back and forth. With most players, most of the time, points are generally over in 2-4 shots.

Your first priority, no matter what, is to keep the ball in play. If you hit your return of serve into the net, or out, the point is over. If you double fault your serve, you never even created any challenge for your opponent.

Maybe, you are trying too hard to end points too soon by going for winners. Hitting winners feels great, but if most of your attempts at winners don't make it, you are trying too hard. Hit higher over the net, leave yourself a larger margin of error. Hitting a ball one foot inside the line is a lot better than one inch inside the line, even if it looks "terrific". (Inside, you know you are being lucky when the ball just drops in).

Think of challenging your opponent, not blowing him off the court. You might want to try to make sure you hit two balls per point, and then three balls. In most cases, if you can hit three balls per point, you'll find that you are winning the game. In any case, you are definitely challenging your opponent if you can hit three balls per point most of the time.

Sometimes you'll feel almost defeated. Your opponent's shot has pulled you way off the court. Still, if at all possible, you might as well make your opponent hit one more ball before giving up. He might not even expect the ball to come back and not watch it carefully and make an error.... Of course, sometimes there'll be no way for you to get to your opponent's shot. Then just think, well done. Let's go to the next point.

2. Playing your game

It's easier to keep the ball in play with shots you know how to make than with shots you haven't mastered yet. This again sounds very fundamental, but in the heat of the game it is not always possible to live up to this principle.

The big difference between hitting shots in practice and during games and matches is the amount of effort you give to get into position for the shot.

In practice, you will hit a lot of balls without having to work hard at getting into position, because you are given, or only "go for" balls that are relatively easy to get to.

During games and matches, the opposite occurs. Your opponent will try to challenge you by hitting shots you are not in position for. In other words, you have to move more and will be tempted to reach shots even if you are not in a proper position to execute the shot.

There is a common expression of the player who is able to play "within" himself. This means that he is able to use, most of the time, shots he feels comfortable executing. People who come back from a good outing will realize that they were able to play within themselves. During a match it is not possible to always play a comfortable shot. There will be times you will be stretched, and you still should try to get the ball back. But the more shots you play comfortably, the more balls you will get back, and if you can get back three or more balls per point, you will be winning your share of matches. Better still, you will have fun.

The idea of "reaching the shot" is to put yourself in position to execute a shot you are able to make. In fact, the better you are able to be in position, the more you are able to control the point, and the better the chance that you will force an error from your opponent.

A key ingredient in this process is anticipation. Great tennis players never seem to be out of position because they "know" sooner than others where their opponent is going put his next shot. But average players can anticipate as well. The first step is to "know" that your opponent will return the ball. Don't watch to see "if" he will return your shot. *Expect the ball to come back.* Start moving to your next position.

Next, you watch your opponent's movement, racket swing and how the ball comes off his racket and adjust your movement to meet the ball. Small quick steps are much more effective than large paces.

The overall goal is to reach the shot by putting yourself in position, so you are able to execute a shot you feel comfortable making. It sounds so simple, but it never is, because where you need to be is in part determined by your opponent's shot.

3. Focus

One big difference between great tennis players and everyone else is that they are better able to focus their mind on the game, actually on the point being played than others. They are capable at suppressing whatever can distract them from the game. In addition, they're often also better at sustaining this level of concentration much longer than average players. No one can keep a high level of concentration up continuously, but those who can do it more and longer are at a definite advantage.

Some people with incredible talent for the game, and who can look spectacular during practice, don't have the ability to maintain their concentration through the duration of a match, and perennially disappoint themselves with their match results.

Recreational players should look at the idea of focus as something to strive for, and to correct for, when errors are creeping into their game during a match.

The more you are able to focus on the ball and your opponent, the more of a challenge you are to your opponent, and the more fun you'll have.

It's very hard to ignore all distractions. There are distractions from things happening on or around the court. Players in the court next to you, or people around the court may be distracting. Short conversations with your opponent between games may stick in your mind.

The opportunities for the mind to wander are endless. On court, our minds just have the tendency to go all over the place, replaying the previous point, thinking about what will happen if I don't win this point, where we are going for dinner tonight, etc.

Some people enhance their ability to focus by breathing calmly between points. Those who practice yoga and meditation learn to guide their wandering minds back to the point of focus.

We don't need a whole theory or philosophy about how to learn to focus better. For the average tennis player there is ample opportunity to use focus in match play *by realizing when you are not focusing enough.*

When you miss an easy volley, or when your shots keep hitting the top of the net instead of going over, you should ask yourself how well you are concentrating.

One of the easiest things to try is this: Watch the ball longer! Coaches often tell us to watch the ball all the way onto our strings, but, frankly, that seems impossible. First try to watch the ball longer. That means, see it sooner, and keep watching it longer before hitting it. The mental effort involved in that is enough to help raise your level of concentration.

The second common piece of advice is to only think of the point you are playing right now, not the previous point, and not the next point.

How often, serving at 30-0, are you already thinking of the ace you are going to try to hit at 40-0? What's likely to happen is that you don't make it to 40-0 and will be serving at 30-15 instead.

And how often, when you miss a return of serve, do you realize you were still thinking of what happened in the previous point?

Put other points out of your mind and focus on the point you are playing right now.

4. Making small adjustments

When things don't go perfect during a match, and they rarely do, you should consider making some adjustments. Sometimes, the cross-court forehand you always hit with ease keeps going wide. Sometimes, too many of your return of serves are going out. After 5-6 games, and certainly after losing the first set, it may be time to consider making a few adjustments. Don't keep doing the same thing over and over.

An adjustment is a change to your game plan. It isn't a small thing you try just once to see if it works. It is a conscious adjustment you apply to your game for a while, to see if you have better results. It takes some "sticking to" a new approach to prove it works. You may not execute your adjustment well right away, so you should give yourself a few chances to get the adjustment right.

The following are examples of small adjustments. Over time you will learn which adjustments are most effective in your own game. Sometimes, opponent's play (and their success against you) will create a need for an adjustment. For example, the adjustment against a hard hitter is different than the adjustment you have to make against a dinker who puts a lot of spin on the ball.

Slow down a bit:

This idea again is so fundamental that we often forget we have it at our disposal. Rushing your game is a quick way to let your errors multiply. An opponent who rushes you can also be the kind of distraction that causes you to make more errors than necessary.

So slow down. Take a bit more time to pick up the balls, getting in position for the next point, thinking where you want to put your next serve. Try to breathe slowly, and if you have to catch your breath between points, take the time for it.

You can also slow down your strokes a bit, so long as you hit the ball deep into the court. (See the next point)

Hit higher over the net:

Hitting higher over the net has several great benefits. You lower the chance that you will actually hit the net, and, more likely than not, when you hit the ball with good clearance over the net, it will land deeper on your opponent's side of the court, which makes it harder for him to hit a good shot back to you again. (You may, of course, have to adapt your swing if every ball goes out, by slowing down your stroke, or by putting more topspin on the ball).

Hit more balls cross-court:

The court is longer cross-court, and, everything else being equal, you may have more success at hitting the ball with good clearance over the net, and in, when you hit cross-court. The net is actually a bit lower in the center, so why not use that more often to your advantage?

Hitting cross-court is also a good way to make your opponent move, and/or to force him to make the harder down-the-line shot.

Shorten your swing:

When you are hitting a lot of balls out, or when you have trouble returning your opponent's serve, try shortening your stroke. By shortening your swing, you give yourself more time to get the moment of impact "right".

It is still important to keep good form when you shorten your swing. When you make your swing more compact, you still should be in as good a position as possible to make the shot, use your entire arm and shoulder, and move your body into the shot. But there is less of a follow-through, so you can get yourself ready for the next ball a split-second faster than if you allowed your arm to make a complete follow-through.

Get more first serves in:

We all know we are supposed to get our first serve in. It creates opportunities. The point is, if you miss too many of your first serves, you should make an adjustment. What do you need to do to get more of your first serves in?

This adjustment is a personal matter. The most obvious solution is to hit the ball at 70-80% of your normal first serve speed to find your accuracy. Some people go to hitting only second serves. Some people just put more spin on their serves to get greater clearance over the net. The point is, you need to have a way to get more of your first serves in on the day that the normal routine isn't working. You owe it to yourself, and you owe it to your opponent.

Hit some short balls:

When you play someone who is beating you most of the time in rallies, it is a good idea to make that person move up and down as well as back and forth across the base line. Short balls are tricky, because if you make it too easy on your opponent, they are an invitation to him to hit a winner. So try to make your opponent move to get to your short ball. Even if he gets it, you have put him on notice that you have some surprises in store for him, and this already may help. In any case, you have given him another form of a challenge.

5. Patience

In almost any match between recreational tennis players, actually all tennis players, there are going to be fluctuations in intensity and success. Come to think of it, the "ebb and flow" of who seems to be in control during a match is one the fun things about tennis. It takes quite a number of points to win a set, and quite a lot more again to win two sets. In that quest, you and your opponent are going to be wavering in the degree of control you have over each other.

When things are not going well for you in a match, there is one thing you can be quite sure of. Your opponent will not play at the same level all the way through. He will be distracted, or he will relax. If you make two or three points in a row, no matter what the score, you have established your challenge for the moment. Even if your opponent is up 5-1, there's pressure to finish a set. So, don't give it away.

Patience, not losing your composure, is a great asset in tennis. Cultivate it, and use it. It is yet another way to give your recreational opponent the challenge he deserves. And when you create a challenge for your opponent, you'll taste the fun of competition.

7

Strategy and Tactics

Driven by the genetic nature of our human potential we tend to think that winning is the only thing. But it is clear that the human race's highest survival values be in intelligence, a moral sense and cooperation.

How we play the game may turn out to be more important than we imagine for it signifies nothing less than the way of being in the world, and the important decision in life for recreation lies in "creative play", the experience of a player placed in an open environment using his imagination to devise forms of play.

Tennis is that part of many people's human endeavor giving emphasis to their human potential. The decisions that we make should center in the joy of playing cooperation and trusting rather than survival just to win. We must create an atmosphere through our own decision that encourages spontaneity and participation.

The joyous and harmonious interaction between people on the tennis court makes them aware of themselves. Fun now becomes a great "decision" and a new game in itself. It, therefore, becomes the number one decision and most strategic as we approach the game we all enjoy.

Tactics in tennis are the methods of playing and positioning that you use to in your strategic plan of improvement. New techniques of play and, oftentimes, new equipment add a refinement to your play when you go on the attack.

Although tactics play a major part of your strategy, one of the greatest secrets of outstanding performance in tennis is learning to focus and to concentrate on each point.

Always remember that strategy in tennis must depend on your own strengths in attack, defense and counter-attack. Challenge your opponent and attack with accurate, strong strokes at every opportunity.

There are a number of basic types of players you must learn to recognize and deal with. Based on your analysis you must plan to your counter attack according to the issues you are presented with.

Issue: THE RETRIEVER:

The retriever relies on his strength to scramble to get the ball back with precision and consistency. They hustle down shots attempting to get you to over-hit and make errors.

Tactics to use:

1. Don't get lured into hitting winners—hit down the middle to avoid his angles
2. Create opportunities to rush the net and put away attempting to shorten the point
3. Hit short angles bringing him to the net so you can pass
4. Hit the ball back where it came from keeping the ball in play several times until you can take charge and attack
5. Move your opponent from side to side and hit behind him
6. Don't force anything—causing errors

Issue: THE SLOW PLACEMENT SERVER

The slow placement server generally will be perceived as having a weak serve. However, he makes up his lack of pace on the serve with good placement. It is easy to over-hit your returns.

Tactics to use:

1. Keep your errors down by returning the serve back to where it came from. Don't change direction of the ball all the time

2. Move up to return service.

3. Don't get lazy. Move your feet by making small steps of adjustment to put your body in the best position to hit your return smoothly.

4. Approach the net on the return, and put the return deep into the court

5. Vary drop shots and angles to both sides

Issue: THE GREAT FOREHAND DRIVER

An opponent with a great forehand is a challenge, because it means the ball will be struck consistently with pace, depth, spin and angles from his forehand side. The overall goal is to not let this person get into a "groove", by making him move, so he has little or no time to set up for the shot.

Tactics to use:

1. Hit wide to the forehand side

2. Give him a short ball on the backhand, followed by a lob

3. Vary your depth: Hit long and short balls, use drop shot slices

4. Hit lobs and looping balls to change the pace of the point

5. Come in on your own serve when he doesn't expect it, to force him to hit a better return.

Issue: THE (GOOD) VOLLEYER

The good volleyer likes to come to the net, because he has confidence in the shot. He likes to put his opponent on the defense by rushing him. Volleyers expect to miss a certain number of points at the net. The challenge is to disrupt his confidence a bit, by making him miss more than usual, and to make it harder for him to get to the net.

Tactics to use:

1. Hit cross-court returns so you can capitalize on your angles

2. Move back a bit but catch the ball on the rise

3. Use slice and topspin, vary your pace

4. Lob to both corners

Issue: THE "CHOPPER"

The chopper hits many balls with a slice back spin or side spin. Again, the goal of your tactics is to not let this person get into a "groove":

1. Come to the net with decisive pace and depth to your shots

2. Slice the ball back at an angle

3. Hit soft drop shots

4. Keep the ball in play—Move him from side to side

5. Hit high deep shots close to the baseline

6. Don't get too close to the net when attacking, watch out for the lob

Issue: THE LEFTY CRUSHER

Playing left-handed opponents can be tricky, especially if they have a good serve that curves in the opposite way than we are used to from right handed opponents. It is harder to anticipate what a left handed player will hit to you, so it takes extra concentration and intensity to play a left handed opponent.

Tactics to use:

1. Observe what side your opponent favors, finds easiest to hit from, already during warm-up. Try to cover up your own weaknesses

2. Don't hit too hard

3. Move your feet: Avoid hitting off balance

4. Don't over-hit the service returns, think placement and depth before power

5. Use the lob on the return of serve, or

6. Hit the service return on the rise.

Remember to always have a game plan. Also, be able to adjust your game to your opponent's weaknesses. But don't get "lured" into changing your plan by your opponent. Stay mentally in control of what you are trying to do.
Play with intensity and focus, do think, but don't berate yourself.
Do not underestimate your opponent. Instead, have fun and build your confidence as you stay in control of your plan of attack.

8

Think Doubles Tactics for Fun

A top-flight singles player is not necessarily a great doubles player. The strategy is different and invariably the top volleyers—those with the quickest hands and the ability to know where to place the volley make up the best doubles teams.

Good doubles means taking the offense and jamming the net, which puts pressure on the opponents. Doubles is action-packed and a tremendous challenge to the mental and physical ability of the players. Doubles develops in the players a fiery spurt of fun and competition vital to any success on the court.

The server is very important. He should always try to get his first serve in the court and follow his serve to the net as much as possible. It is impossible to overemphasize the importance of hitting your first serve in and coming to the net. The great majority of all winning doubles shots are made from the net position. This makes the net really a two-to-one advantage over playing from the baseline position.

Taking the offense at every opportunity is a "must" and should be practiced until it becomes second nature. Play at the net is incredibly fast and takes great footwork hitting the ball in front of your body.

The net player must think every shot is coming to him and be alert and in proper position. Proper position play requires talking to your partner offering encouragement and assistance getting into position and a killing mode for the execution of winning shots.

Keep focused with your brain reflexes sharp and make tactical returns in split seconds. Quickness and excellent balance are necessary to be in the best position for the best exchange. Practice and match experience are the answer to those challenges.

The most productive shot at the net is the deep volley or the lower volley at the feet of your opponents. Clearly it is the most profitable to have in your arsenal of sharply angled strokes.

Many net strokes are used as tactical weapons to force the opponent out of position. A good goal is to force the opponents to volley upward. This means that, once the opponents are drawn out of position or forced to hit a weak shot, the alert net player takes the advantage by pounding an angle shot for a clean placement.

The exact position and distance from the net should be determined by the height and speed of reaction of the players, including the force of the serves of each particular player.

In many cases, the players can be as close to the net as their ability to protect against the lob will allow.

At the very top level of doubles play, the most important and effective factors are quick reflexes, a great volley, a confident overhead, a lob, solid return of serve and the ability to get one's first serve in 80-90 percent of the time.

Practice tactical skills and moves with emphasis on poaching early in your scheme of doubles practice.

There are a number of considerations that will help you decide when or how to approach coming to the net behind serve against one or both opponents in a specific situation.

If you are a weak volleyer, it becomes more difficult to come in behind the serve, especially against very strong opponents. Practice your serve and volley against players of your own level to gain confidence in following your serve into the net.

If you are only a fair volleyer, or if you have trouble focusing well on a particular day, or your footwork feels suspect, then come in only against the receiver who is returning the ball hitting up, or otherwise not forcing you. Don't come in on an opponent who is knocking the cover off the ball, or who is making you dive or lunge for the ball, or trapping you with low shots at your feet.

Remember, if you are a good volleyer, but one opponent is ripping you badly with his returns, stay back and come in off his second return, or his third or fourth shot.

If an opponent is lobbing your weaker partner (at the net) and you are forced to cover lobs try an Australian Formation: This is where your partner stand in the service box in front of the server, and the server comes to the net on the opposite diagonal.

If you find you are successful coming in behind first serve, but one opponent is stepping around his backhand and hitting strong forehands off your second serve, stay back on the second serve and then come in on a shorter shot return.

If you are an average-to-above average volleyer but volleyed poorly some returns of both opponents, don't retreat to staying back. Rather, change your serving tactics. For example, it may be possible to serve wide to the opponent's forehand and come in, because the opponent going for a wide serve will probably give a weak return on which you can groove your volleys. Keep looking for returning weaknesses in your opponents. Only if there are none should you retreat to staying back on your serve.

Observe and evaluate the return of serve patterns that will make it easier for you to get into position for a winning shot. Always be careful of the player who has an erratic style of return, or the one who is very hard to predict. He will force you into unnecessary errors. Be mindful to observe and evaluate your opponents.

Perhaps your partner is an outstanding volleyer and you are just a little tentative at the net. In that case you should encourage your partner to make poaching moves to throw your opponents off balance and the receiver into hitting up to you on your approach.

Most of the time a good receiver, when faced with an opponent who can poach will go for the sharp cross-court return. So, follow your serve in with that in mind. They are creating your strategy for making them play your game.

So the name of the game in doubles is to come in on your serve. It will add depth to your game. Work on your first serve and first volley.

Placement of the serve is much more important than power. The first serve should have some depth. And try to serve to the other players' weakness on either side or directly into his body.

It is important not to volley on the dead run. So, serve, run forward, then stop, punch your first volley, and then take two more steps in, i.e. "jamming" the net.

Always remember to punch the ball out in front of you. Stay focused on watching the ball hit your racket. Anytime you are in doubt about where the punch volley should go, go for depth down the center of the court. Aim for deep volleys low over the net.

Each ball that comes right at you to the center of your body should be taken on your backhand. Don't jump sideway to hit a forehand volley. With a backhand volley you will get punch out in front by turning your body and shoulders and stepping toward the net.

Follow the ball as it comes off your opponent's racket and move in the line of the return. Use your eyes to determine where the ball is going and react. Take the volley at its highest point and keep moving into the net. This creates less time for your opponents and puts them in a defensive position.

Crowding the net is the "Mother of all attack" in doubles and puts enormous pressure on your opponents.

Many times a half volley will be useful when you come in to the net. It is important to cut down on the backswing of a half volley, but do use a smooth and firm follow through.

Take time to practice volleys and half volleys to become a good, solid doubles player.

The "One up-one back" Formation

Although aggressive net play is essential for high-level play in doubles, many recreational players cannot serve or volley well enough to come in on every serve with confidence. Many high school players have these limitations as well.

This does not mean that these players cannot win at doubles at their level of play. If you are teamed properly with a partner with compensating skills you can devise tactics that permit the team to make the best use of each other's abilities. This should give them a chance to play effectively.

Each team should devise a set of tactics that will permit them to operate within their own capabilities. These tactics need not imitate the very top-flight players. It should be the strategy that is best for their particular team: Using the special talents of each player while avoiding weak and error-prone shots.

There are many variations, but the most common would be the "one up, one back" formation.

The basic idea of this formation is to allow the good driver on the team to play from the backcourt with his consistency and follow through, pulling the team into an effective attack, punctuated by his partner who is at the net and can hit great short volleys.

This formation turns the backcourt into the main base of operations. After serving and the return you stay at the baseline and utilize the strength of your offensive returns. Likewise, you also stay back after return of your opponents' serve.

Determine your approach to the net by coming in on short balls only, and then attack safely.

Accuracy is the key and placement the important factor as the baseliner keeps his drives away from the opposing net man. If his opponent gets very good at poaching he may have to rely on a great lob.

Most players who can rally from the baseline can develop an accurate lob. The lob can also be a factor in return of service. Using it as a form of attack or a surprise tactic.

In the "one up, one back" formation we must emphasize that the back player's chief function is to protect his partner in several ways depending on the opponent's position.

Actually, if the opposing team is also in the "one up, one back" formation, drive deep to the other baseliner. If both are at the net, then drive low to the player who is farther back, at the weak player or over the center of the net. When in doubt, always hit down the middle.

When playing one up, one back, the person working the baseline also has the important role to go on the offensive when a safe opportunity presents itself. He can aim deep at the other baseline player or right at the net man to force an error. Always try to attack the net person when he is off-balance and can't defend himself.

When you are in the intermediate level of doubles play, you use the lob to get yourself out of trouble. Especially when the opponent poaches successfully, it is very useful to lob over him. The more the opposing net person bothers your side, the more you should try to lob him and to hit down the line in the alley. You want to restrict and discourage his poaching moves and leave more room for your angles and drives. Lob to the person with the weakest overhead.

When receiving service in middle class of doubles play, a lob can be effective especially on the right side where the weaker receiver is usually stationed and the opposing net man is eager to approach. A lob that will clear the net man on his half of the court completely disrupts the attacking team. The purpose is to keep the ball as far away as possible from the opposing poacher. He will often become impatient waiting to poach and roam out of his pre-arranged territory. This gets them off balance causing errors. This is common when a strong player is combined with a weaker player. Take advantage of the weaker player.

The net man in the one up, one back offense may sometimes play up-close to the net, or three to four feet away. If his partner can hit deep and keep the opposing team off balance, he can play close and jam the net being always on his toes to react quickly. (He must always be ready to defend himself regardless).

When he senses the opponents are in trouble he should move up to anticipate a weak return, and the opportunity for an easy put-away. On the other hand, he may have to retreat sometimes to the baseline to play defense when his partner lobs.

As the net man you must know what your partner is doing and notice his position on the court and be able to anticipate his intentions. Briefly watch your partner's reactions to play, but only briefly. Be alert to move forward, backward or to either side. Defend your half of the court at all times. When your partner is forced wide into the alley, you should move more into the middle of the court into a defensive position to close off angles your opponents can take advantage of.

It is important to watch your partner, but you must focus as much on the opposing net man and his moves.

Serving Strategies

Always talk to your partner and give encouragement. When any of the following situations arise, you should discuss these serving strategies.

It may be that the server is not effective enough to put pressure on the receiver, but only hits the serve well enough to put the ball in play. Regardless, the server should aim his serve at the opponent's weakest side, which is usually the backhand.

The positions of the server become very important when playing in the one up, one back formation. When serving from the right (deuce) court, the server should stand close to the center mark. This gives him a strategic straight down the line shot to the receiver's backhand.

If unable to serve to the receiver's backhand, the server should stand over toward the sideline. This forces the receiver to expose more of the court on his backhand side than he did on serves from near the center.

The server can then move a step or two toward his left to protect his own backhand from the receivers return. When serving from that position the server is provided with a convenient target formed by the center service line, center strap and the service line. Sometimes wide serves can also be effective if the receiver is covering his backhand too much.

If you are serving from the left (ad) court, the most effective location from which to hit to the receiver's backhand is close to the alley. From there he can make a diagonal shot to the corner. When the opponent starts to lob he can move his position closer to the center mark in an attempt to control the play to go on the attack. Sometimes it's effective to split half way—a decision you can make as the match progresses.

First serves at all levels of play are the most important basic element of play even if hit at medium speed. An occasional hard serve is necessary to keep the opponent guessing. Good depth on the service is most important on both serve attempts. Work on placement.

The net man should always encourage the server as his partner. Use a variation of serving formations matched to the skills of your team. Work from your strengths and adopt a series of signals from the net man to the server. For example, a clinched fist to signal your intent to poach and an open hand for staying in your position.

The server recognizes the signal and moves accordingly. The server can give a gesture if necessary that he recognizes the attack the team is attempting. This promotes team spirit and an effective purpose for each point. It helps the team to stay focused.

Often, the stronger player of the opposing team receives serves in the left (ad) court. A common strategy to prevent the left court receiver from driving to the server's backhand is the Australian formation. For this, the server stands close to the center mark to serve. His partner should station himself on the same side of the center line at the net and face the receiver head-on. The thinking here is to force the receiver to hit his return away from the net man, to the server's forehand. The server moves over quickly, after having served, to be in position to play the return on his forehand. He is then in a great position to hit forehands. Balls aimed at his backhand are likely to be within reach of his net man who is able to capitalize on a strong forehand volley.

Other Tactics

Another innovation of doubles play taking advantage of the strong points of the game of your team is when the stronger player on your team rushes the net on every serve and also on all his returns of service.

Remember to adjust your game when the team is not doing well on the attack. The partner can start and remain in the backcourt, or attack as a team.

The weaker server should serve from the right court with the strong player should standing close to the center mark and dashing quickly to this left to volley. His partner may stand to the right of him throughout the point. From that position he is able to use his stronger forehand on almost all balls hit to his half of the court.

When serving from the left court, the strong player runs straight to the volley while his partner stays back. This can be a very different alignment but can be very effective on the attack play.

You can adjust your team so that in some situations only one player really comes to the net, with the other one playing defense protecting his partner and setting him up for put aways. The partner who is back roams the court setting up his partner for kill shots. This is a great attack for high school doubles teams adjusting their strengths in to the attack.

Choosing Positions To Attack From

When you form doubles combinations you must decide who plays which side of the court. When one player is likely to be weaker or less aggressive, the logical place to put him is in the right court. Mainly he is less likely to have to return the serve with his backhand because it is more difficult for most servers to place the ball there than when serving to the left court.

Following his serve, many balls returned to his backhand can be played by his partner with the forehand. This is true whether the team is at the net or in the backcourt. When you are in the backcourt there is almost always time for the left court player to drift over and take more than his percentage of balls and hit to the center. It is also an important formation for being at the receiving end of lobs, because the strong player can manage to get a forehand smash on most lobs.

Another plan to protect the weaker player if he has the ability to volley reasonably well is to put him at the net where he can hit forehand volleys. He takes up a position on the left side closer to the sideline and closer to the net than the regular net man may play. He should take all shots on his forehand volley a strategy that could appeal to the high school coach who must have a game plan that fits a strategy of utilizing only a handful of strengths leaving little room for the player to face backhands. He becomes a strong volleyer because he is on top of the net—so the opponents find out early to keep the ball away from him. This may also be a good strategy for mixed doubles.

The stronger player covers the largest share of the court and hits deep always protecting the net man. To play the strong position requires a great amount of anticipation, agility and good footwork. This is a great tactic when your doubles teams are thin with aggressive players. This worked well when I coached in high school and we had to the meet with the matches in the doubles events. Doubles became our strongest suit and players became confident looking forward to the competition and good emphasis to their play.

The most effective way to play doubles for the great teams is to begin in the one up, one back position with one player in the volley position and his partner moves up to join the attack on both serve and return of serve. It is easy to move into a parallel attack from this formation also as you move equally distances as an attacking team—you must talk together and encourage each other.

The player who hits the ball decides the attack action of the team. The partner watches closely and follows his indication of the attack move. If the hitter decides not to rush the net his partner can stay back to play a defensive position. If neither player can volley well they may be in a parallel defense and develop their attack together getting everything back and down the middle.

The lob becomes an essential part of your defense and should be directed with purpose. If one of your opponents is too close to the net, lob over his head. Lob to the weaker opponent when he is in close and you can find direction to the weaker player or the shorter player.

When in doubt hit down the middle, but during the warm-up decide who will get most of your returns. Lob diagonally cross-court which gives you a better percentage. This can be especially effective when the lobber is hitting from the alley or from outside the court.

Try to cause confusion among your opponents when you are on the defense. Have a game plan for doubles and adjust it as you go from set to set, especially as you discover weaknesses in the armor of your opponents. Doubles tactics are most effective if you base your game plan on your strengths, but being mindful of your opponents' weaknesses is almost as useful.

Mixed Doubles: The Fun Tactics of Give and Take

The game of mixed doubles is a lot of fun and can be a great social and recreational activity. It is a tremendous give-and-take experience, built around teamwork. Working together keeping pressure on your opponents is always the basic axiom.

There are many delightful aspects. It should never challenge or destroy the fundamental relationship between a man and a woman. Many women are extremely athletic and terrific partners. In many cases they are the better of the team members. The team should operate as a unit remaining side by side in attacking the net or scrambling in the backcourt. Remember even in fun doubles, the attacking team has the advantage.

The cardinal principle of the mixed doubles game is working together to reach the net. The net is where you win your points and is the heart of the action.

There are some considerations that should help you decide whether you should come in behind serve.

In almost all top doubles matches the server follows his serve to the net. Whether you should or should not depends upon your own ability and the extent your opponent can take advantage of any of your weaknesses. If you can't win by following serve to the net every time then your alternative may be to come in behind your second shot or behind the first short ball.

In certain matches the opponents have different returns of serve. One player may hit only a medium return of serve that you can volley decisively. If your other opponent catches you with low returns then stay back on the first serve. Evaluate your opponents. Find a groove to get into for the team to score. If you are a weak volleyer don't come in behind serve against strong opponents. Perhaps you are a fair volleyer but your eyes are not focusing, you are slow on you feet then only come in only against the weaker opponent.

If you opponents are lobbing your weaker partner then stay back or try the Australian Formation.

Your partner may be a fine volleyer and you are slightly tentative at net but your partner's poaching may rattle the other teams into hitting up to you and always cross-court. Come in if you know the direction the ball is coming.

Make your serve deep and very well placed, hitting the first serve in as you serve to the opponent's weakness.

Never stop to let ball drop, keep moving to hit the volley at its highest point.

Focus yopur eyes on the ball as it comes off the opponent's racket and move in the line of its return. You must know where the ball is going. Turn your shoulders or move in one step but never hit the volley on a dead run.

Don't take a backswing on the volley and keep that punch out in front of you. Use a half-volley when appropriate and keep a firm follow-through. Focus on the ball.

Start with your strongest tactical server taking a position midway between the center of the baseline and the doubles sideline thus leaving a shorter route to a proper position at the net. Position your partner in a position midway between the net and service line and 10 feet away from the far side-line.

Most important is to get the first serve in. Using a three-quarter-speed serve is very effective, because it allows the server to get several steps closer into the net than would be possible if you try hitting a flat cannonball service.

The poach is a most vital play in mixed doubles because it becomes a shot decided by the team and in most cases is decided by signals from each service situation.

If opponents have taken control of the net, mixed doubles teams should attempt to get back on the offense with the lob. This is an excellent strategic movement and will drive the opponents back. Be careful not to come in on too short of a lob. Whenever possible place the offensive lob to the backhand side of either of your opponents. Not very many players can hit a forceful overhead from the backhand side. Communicate and go on the offense to the net.

Ron's Golden Rules for Mixed Doubles

MEN	WOMEN
1. Always play your best. Most women are allergic to losing.	1. Compliment your partner when he makes a great shot.
2. Ask your partner whether they would like to serve first.	2. Don't apologize when you miss.
3. When it's time for your team to receive stand firmly in left court and ask her which side she would like.	3. Wear a great outfit—intriguing for your opponents.
4. Never use the word "bitch" during the match.	4. Let your partner serve first.
5. If ball goes over the fence run and get it immediately—women don't like lazy men.	5. Don't interact or gossip with other players or people walking by. Be quiet but communicate with your partner.
6. Don't play the female opponent all of the time, but decisively when you do. It's rewarding to win.	6. Don't make your partner fetch all the loose balls.
7. When your partner calls a ball incorrectly don't correct her.	7. Always play your best—men prefer to win.

9

The Amateur Tennis Tournament Experience

Certainly a psychologist could find cases to document all of their theories of personality by spending a long weekend at the local tennis courts as an amateur tournament takes place.

In the course of a few hours he would observe many different forms of behavior and misbehavior. Emotions become tense as rackets and balls fly about the local premises, into the net, off net post, and over the fences.

The pressure rises as the line-ups are posted on the court fences. Players and their parents or loved ones try to visualize and contemplate where they will be when the sun sets, and the court lights are turned on for the extended late matches.

Amateur tennis tournaments are the ultimate tennis experience, the chance for youngsters and adults to dream about what it would be like to be a pro. It's fun to let your emotions carry you to the fantasy of stardom. Enjoying the experience of an amateur tournament builds confidence, teaches sportsmanship, and contributes a sense of what life and growing up is all about.

Junior amateur tournaments offer a whole range of social experiences, whether it be skinny-dipping in the moonlight, or walking through a scary cemetery. It can be sharing a pop and candy, or comparing school experiences. An important topic of conversation is the next junior tournament, and who will be there. Sharing a tournament picnic. A highlight can be staying overnight at gracious patrons of the tournament who lavish kindness on those participants who have traveled from afar.

Patrons are an important group of adults who find pleasure in kindly furnishing a great experience for traveling youngsters, acting as the parent away from home. Patrons may also contribute to tournaments by organizing and supervising satellite tournament sites.

Tournament directors, club presidents and junior participants hold patrons in high esteem. Tournament patrons open their home and, in most cases, their hearts to the visiting kids. Unfortunately, there are never enough adults to contribute this important experience for the kids. In Dubuque, Iowa, a small town on the Mississippi River, this experience still flourishes during the month of July, and it might provide great experience for a hopeful junior player.

We should always encourage participation in amateur tournaments. It is the greatest tennis experience available to non-professional players. There are literally thousands of them held at clubs, indoor courts and public parks, in cities everywhere. The tournaments may involve state rankings or the championship of an age group, club or almost anything else. Most amateur tournaments are open to all who care to pay the entry fee, which is usually in the $8-15 range.

Entry in a tournament entitles you to play a role in a tennis drama and a chance to see a different side of tennis than casual play offers.

Tournaments are usually held over a weekend for adults and for three consecutive weekdays for juniors. It is a time of thinking of matches, draw sheets, scores, seeded players and a constant feeling of whom-do-I-play-next. The outcome of a confrontation with an opponent is really of some consequence in the tournament setting. Many times it provides a rather significant point in players' tennis lives, symbolizing the highest point many amateurs can reach. It makes you think of goals and a plan for your tennis life.

It is the closest many kids and adults will get to the "thrill of victory and the agony of defeat". There is a chance here to indulge in the fantasy of what living the life of a tennis pro is like. The players are completely immersed in the tournament and the dream is a reality for as long as the players last in the tournament. Until a player loses he is an equal of all other survivors—a situation that creates a shared experience among those present. Friendship and camaraderie are forged as players strive for the common goal. They use many of the same strategies and shots to try to attain their goal, and many have the same fear and apprehension as they face competition.

As you may spend as much as ten hours in a day playing tennis under the sun, filled with both the worries and excitement, a special bond develops between you and your partner and other players that may be comparable to crossing a desert together, or climbing Mount Everest.

Eventually, most dedicated tennis players start to take their tennis more seriously than the average everyday player. They believe that winning a match or two in a tournament will somehow lend credibility to a person's level of play, establishing him (or her) as a bonafide player. The way most tournaments are set up surviving several rounds testifies to your real level of fitness.

We must consider the emotional effects of a loss in a tournament. (Eventually, there is only one winner, everyone else loses somewhere along the way).
The ego-involved player has an obvious letdown, which is usually followed by a hundred excuses why the loss occurred, like "These courts suck, too many cracks and the bounce seemed different". Most don't suffer from such traumatic feelings, and will show their respect to the winner, and rejoice in how far they made it in the tournament.

Many tournaments used to be a haven for the "tennis bums" who went from tournament to tournament. Often such a person would be a part-time teaching pro in the summer, and had the background of some college playing without ever graduating, now enjoying their ego-building successes in summer tournaments.

For Juniors, tournaments present the stepping stone to college tennis and for young adults trying to improve their game during the summer before returning to college in the fall in hopes of making the top six on their school's tennis team.

There are, of course, juniors whose parents have invested thousands of dollars in their kids' tennis development, with hopes of lifting them to the level of headlines in the local paper and/or champion of their age group at their local club. The risk here is that the name of the game becomes "winning at all cost'. Parents would be wise to have them develop sportsmanship, and strive that the child develops an ability to be a "good" winner, as well as being able to take a loss. No one likes a sore loser.

For the luckiest ones the tennis motivation is more than just fame, trophies, rankings or mentions in the paper. They play for fun, gaining new friends, satisfying a healthy desire for competition.

The amateur tournament may not include the glamour stakes of a pro tennis career, but it can be a highly enjoyable experience for all. In the world of amateur tennis tournaments, dreams and fantasy present a fun challenge. They definitely deserve a place in the development of the person involved. Just remember, as you pursue that fantasy of the ultimate experience, do it "One shot at a time".

10

Introducing Kids to Tennis

There is a growing body of evidence that early childhood experiences do have an impact on what becomes of a youngster's potential in sports, and how much enthusiasm kids feel towards sports.

The years from birth to age six are crucial. This is the period in which the groundwork is laid for children's attitudes towards physical activity. Happiness is a large factor in creating positive attitudes towards sports activities and gamesmanship.

Making it fun and keeping things simple, those are the key guidelines towards nurturing enthusiasm for tennis among children. Children who feel no pressure love to play the game.

Physical development is most critical in achieving later success in tennis. Early on, work on improving skills in a general sense, such as throwing, catching and jumping.

Introduce the tennis court maybe around age 7, but realize that there is no substitute for hitting balls against a wall or the garage door. Don't push too hard, emphasize fun and basic motor skills.

Begin with a short racket, almost paddle size, and praise them for making contact. Make the child feel comfortable in their new sport. Even if the child looks like a promising hitter, wait till age 8, 9 or 10 before turning him or her over to the pro for lessons.

Being the way they are, youngsters don't always want to listen to their parents. Their parents are telling them things all day, and they need a change from this once they are out on the court. So, parents have to watch themselves, and try not to expect too much from the beginners. Too many people are over-taught, and, as a result, overly conscious of details.

Physical skills need to be developed, almost robotically, without engaging the mental and emotional aspects of the game; those come later. The teaching must build a strong desire to improve, with emphasis on focus and concentration.

Playing with Mom and Dad can only go so far in early development. As kids progress they must find a peer group, so they learn to share the desire to improve with others. Those others can be older kids, or peers met through attending recreational programs.

Let them be their own person. There should not be a timetable. Development is unpredictable. Do not set a time schedule for your young player.

Eventually, advance in equipment from the paddle sized racket to a junior size racket. Make it a reward for efforts in improvement.

Playing tennis should actually be very simple. Every little detail on how to hit a forehand isn't as important as finding out the basic elements of the game, and then to create a fun plan to learn it. At the start, the best goal should be "Improvement". Often times when a person starts out to learn to play tennis it becomes a struggle. There's confusion over grips, what to do with your hips, wrists, legs, elbows, knees or shoulders and how to move your feet to stay up with the ball. With children we have to stay away from all these complicated details.

You have to stress that tennis is a game. As a game it requires self-discipline determination, effort, concentration and preparation to give the most enjoyment. So youngsters must be ready to pay the small price of "practice", because it takes practice to get pleasure form the game.

But there is no substitute for having fun. Youngsters must have fun as they develop their stroke production. Try to develop the idea that consistency is the number one goal, being able to keep the ball in play. Build a sense of pride about that priority first, before teaching placement, and last of all, power, hitting hard.

For example, start hitting a lot of balls by bouncing the ball and trying to hit it on the first bounce. Better even, find a flat garage door or a wall and let the kids hit the ball against the wall, so they get a good sense of what it feels like to get the ball on the strings. Work on consistency, keeping the ball in play, letting them get the idea of watching where the ball is going and moving the racket to meet the ball.

Courtesy of Julien's Journal

Courtesy of Julien's Journal

Court Games to Make Learning Fun

The three basic elements kids (and all beginners) need to master are ball sense, movement and racket control.

According to John Newcombe, the 1967 US Open and Wimbledon Champion, "Ball Sense" is the ability to determine, as the ball is coming towards you, where it is going to fall in the court and whether you will take it on your forehand or your backhand.

Newcombe is a master at keeping it simple, telling his students to move to the ball *with room to swing*, ("Movement"), and developing the feeling of the strings hitting the ball in a controlled manner ("Racket control").
Everything in tennis becomes the refinement of these three basics.

With children there are some court games to help them refine these basics, without creating the impression that it is a tedious "practice".

A simple game with a group of kids can create interest and excitement as they begin to show an interest in tennis.

King or Queen of the Court

One old standby is "King or Queen of the Court". It's a terrific group game for little people learning the game, and fun at the same time.

You can make up additional rules, but the basic idea is as follows:

One person is King or Queen. The other players line up at the other side of the net, to participate one at a time; one starts, all others wait their turn.

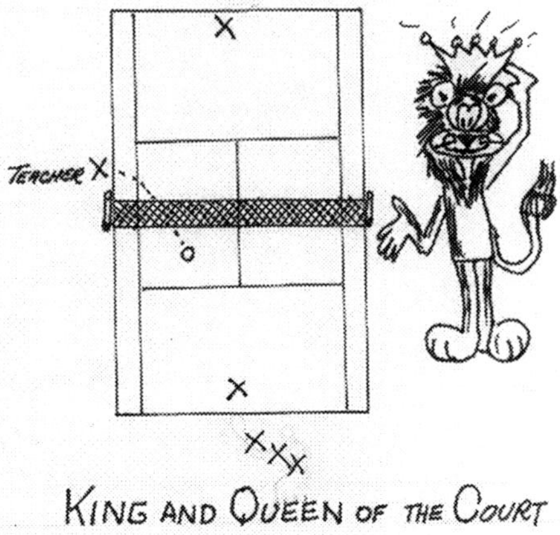

Play begins with the teacher feeding tennis balls from the basket at the netpost to start each rally.

The player on the other side returns the ball, and they rally until an error.

So long as the King or Queen makes no error, he/she remains King/Queen.

Every time the player on the other side makes an error, he or she comes off the court, and the next person takes a turn.

The first person who can force the King/Queen into an error becomes King or Queen. The switch can also be based on the first person who forces the second error off the King/Queen, etc.

It is also possible to create a point system, and keep scores in some way. For example, the King/Queen gets a point for every time he/she scores a point as the king or queen.

With beginner players this game is especially useful if played inside the service lines only, because it teaches consistency, placement and touch, and lowers the temptation to hit the ball hard.

Baseball Tennis

This is another simple group game

Divide the group into two teams.

The coach is the pitcher.

One team is at bat, sending one player at a time into the court. The entire fielding team is on the other side of the net.

TENNIS BASEBALL

The pitcher (teacher) tosses the ball to the batter who must hit the ball on one bounce across the net into the "fielding" team's side of the court. The hit must land inside the singles lines.

If the ball is hit out of bounds or in the net, it's an out.

The fielders position themselves anywhere on their side of the net and must try to hit the ball back on the first bounce. Their return must land inside the doubles lines.

A hit is good when the fielding side makes an error, and the type of hit (single, double, triple or home run) is based on where the last hit landed. (The coach calls the hits).

Players move to the bases and advance as errors are made. Batters cannot be thrown out, they simply advance along the bases.

If the fielders' return is good, the batter gets the next pitch. The "at bat" continues for a total of three-four pitches. If the batter has not been able to get on base, it's an out.

Switch sides after all batters have had a turn, or after 3 outs.

Tennis "Horse"

Divide one side of the court into four target areas and number them.

The players are in line on the other side of the court, taking turns.

The teacher feeds tennis balls from the side of the net post, in a manner to provide maximum control.

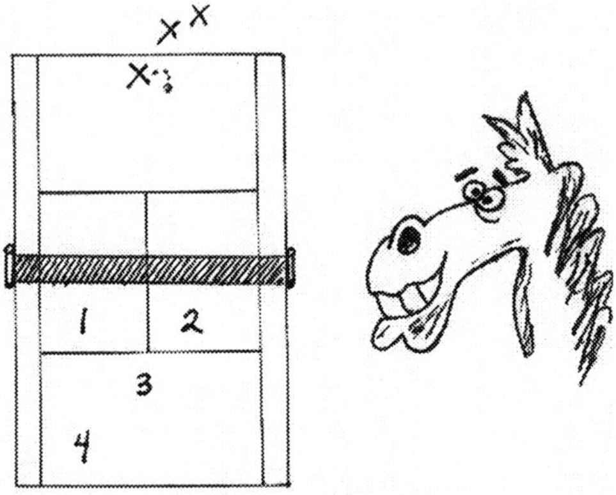

ORDINARY HORSE

The first player up calls "Backhand" or Forehand" and the number of the target area he or she is hitting to. If the shot is good, the next player in line must hit the same shot to the same target.

When a player misses, he or she gets an "H".

The next player in line now can call the shot again (forehand or backhand, and the target area number).

The player who makes a second error gets an "O", etc. After 5 misses a player is eliminated. The winner is the one who is left over after every other player is a "horse."

Relay Tennis

This is a low level game that can be played with a large group of youngsters aimed at ball control.

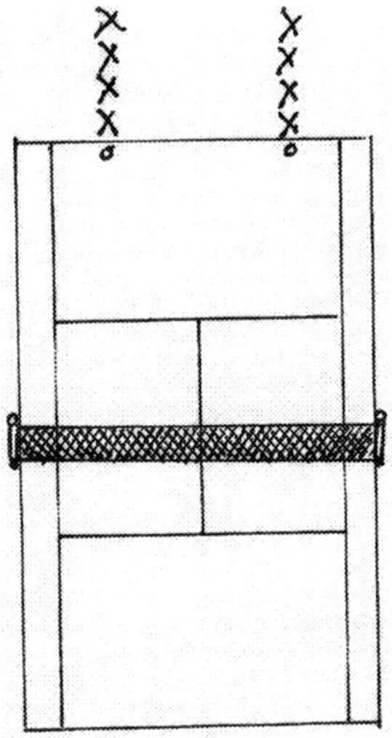

RELAY TENNIS

The group is divided into 2 teams of 6-12 players.

Teams line up at the baseline, side by side.

Each team has a ball. The first player in line will dribble the ball to the net and return. Once the player reaches the service line, he carefully hits it to the next person in line. This player must catch the ball, and then begin his or her dribble to the net.

(A variation of this game could be bouncing the ball on the strings).

The team that completes the relay first is the winner, but the emphasis must be on control, not speed. If players try to complete their relays too quickly they will lose control of the ball, and will lose time as a result.

Throw-catch tennis

Throw-catch tennis is a fun way to help with hand-eye coordination throwing skills, movement, while it also teaches how to score.

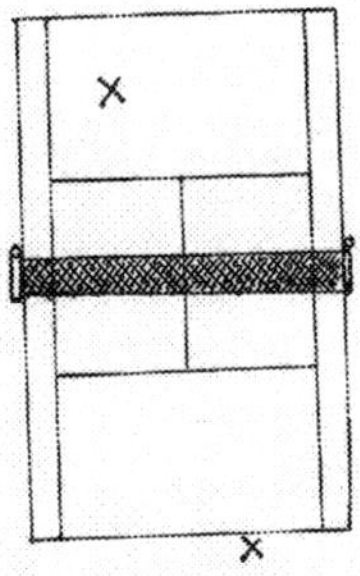

THROW-CATCH TENNIS

Players simulate tennis singles game by throwing (either overhand or underhand) instead of using a racket. The "server" stands in the usual serving position, the receiver can stand anywhere to receive.

The receiver must catch the ball in the air, or on the first bounce. If the receiver catches the ball, then he or she throws the ball into the opponent's court from the spot where the ball is caught.

If a ball isn't caught, or if the ball is thrown out, or into the net, it is an error, and counts as a point.

It is important to use the entire (singles) court in this game, so players get a good sense of moving around, and the opportunities for scoring from different positions in the court.

This game can also be done as a doubles game, once the players have gotten the hang of how to score points.

Traveling the World

Players are divided into equal teams on each side of the court, lining up to take turns at the base line.

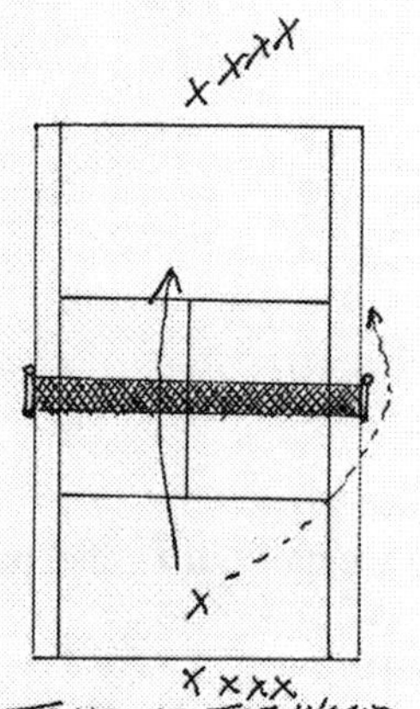
TRAVELING THE WORLD

The first person in one line drops the ball and hits the ball across the net to the first person on the opposite end of the court. He now runs around the right net post the back of the line at the other side of the court.

The objective is to keep the ball in play as long as possible. Unlike other games, no one wins or loses; no one is eliminated for making errors. This is a game to promote teamwork.

This game can also be done in the "short court" (inside the service lines). This is a good version for less experienced players, or to promote "touch" among experienced players.

11

The Role of the "Tennis Parent"

As children have satisfying tennis experiences, they may start to develop pride in their game and this again has a strong impact in their efforts at improvement. Every day is a special day when you are learning and improving. A child should feel free to express himself and capture the thrill of using his developing skills.

All of these great experiences may lead to the desire to compete in tournaments, and to personal goals, such as making the high school or college team. But it remains most important that they have had fun along the way, so that tennis remains a great activity for later in life.

Then primary role of the parent of a budding tennis player is to be supportive, encouraging, interested and caring.

Be understanding and take the pressure of winning off, but be there to correct some behaviors. It is important to get tough with temper outbursts, foul language or cheating. Being tolerant of uncontrolled behavior is a disservice to the child and to the game of tennis.

When a child loses, it is very important to give emotional support and caring. Help them bounce back, which builds self-esteem.

It is a matter of giving support, understanding and encouragement as the young player suffers heartbreaking defeats. The key is to not make these matches a life and death struggle, but to face the reality that tennis is like life itself.

Winning and losing is beyond the control of the parent, but providing a well-rounded personality to face life is very valuable. Help your young tennis player accepting a loss, and dealing with it in an appropriate manner.

"I THINK HE HAS A GOOD CHANCE OF MAKING THE TEAM"

It is important to realize that only a very few, ever, make it to playing professionally for a living. Interim goal making is important for improving your game and chances to climb up the competitive ladder. Such goals might include encouraging the youngster to play above their level to improve. It might be going to a schedule of basic tournaments before high school with the goal of becoming a strong competitor for the high school team. Whatever the direction the youngster is taking, parents need to show their support and positive reinforcement.

When the kids enter competitive junior tennis, being a tennis parent becomes a complex, formidable task.

As you travel around with a group of youngsters, you develop a reputation. Your young player is constantly evaluating what your impact is on the peer group, as well as how you affect your own child.

Emphasize fun and enjoyment. Vary the tennis schedule with relaxing activities like fishing or family outings away from the courts. Some pro's that coach your child will not agree, but remember, tennis is a life time sport, and your youngster can burn out rather quickly with too much of a tennis burden, although this is something to evaluate on an individual basis. Some kids can never get enough tennis.

Do not pressure your player to win. Try to maintain a pressure free climate. Good efforts carry over, so it is much more important to try hard than to actually win.

Encourage your child to play doubles and mixed doubles in tournaments. This can build long lasting friendships.

Young players do not have to dress like the tennis pros and models in Tennis Magazine. Dress comfortably. You do not have to have the most expensive clothes to play strong tennis. The emphasis should be on shoes and a racket that fit your player.

Money is always a factor, but remember that your child's tennis is not a business or financial investment. Don't expect a return on your money as if it were a stock market investment. The return may be in fun and enjoyment. Stretching yourself too thin financially or being strung out mentally, where all you do is traveling around to junior tournaments, will put an unfair burden on your young tennis player. You may have others in your family who need encouragement and support. Make decisions that lead to a healthy, balanced family life.

It is a privilege to win, so don't get too excited either way, whether your youngster is winning or losing. Encourage good sportsmanship. It never hurts to congratulate other parents and their players.

The "hydrogen bomb" of the tennis tournament is when a parent, while watching a match, sees instances of cheating on the opposing team. Parents must stay out of it; they cannot start calling lines or scores. As a parent, you must live with the fact that mistakes do occur. They are bound to happen. It is very hard to hold yourself in, but you must. Your temper-tantrum outburst is much more damaging to your child than for your child learning to live with some unfairness. If it's hard to contain yourself, you should just walk out of the area. It is not wrong to confidentially let the director know what happened from your point of view, but don't bring it up at court itself during a match.

If you look nervous and tense, the same feeling is likely to transfer to your player. Be positive, relaxed, supportive and optimistic. Choose your words carefully. Limit your coaching. Words of encouragement go a long way before a match. You don't know how much this will help your child. The only time when you have to be stern is when your child's behavior (or language) is unacceptable.

Mixing your ego with your child's ego is not a good thing. Don't complicate your child's experience. Remember, you did not play the match. You cannot re-live your own tennis experiences through your children.

As a parent, the relationship with your child's teaching pro is important as well. Your child will always be aware of your reactions and evaluations. Don't go to the lessons on a regular basis, leave the coaching to the coach. Don't take notes or videotape lessons. Such scrutiny can become a negative factor very quickly.

The secret is to not complicate the tennis experience of the youngster. Positive reinforcement and encouragement far out-weigh anything else you might do as the parent of a junior tennis player.

12

Practical Tips

Basic Tennis Etiquette

Many of the important procedures in the game of tennis are not contained in the official rulebook. Anyone new to the game should be encouraged to get out and hit balls for practice. Extensive knowledge of the rules of the game can come later.

Knowledge of the basic ideas of tennis etiquette allows all tennis players to be comfortable working out without any fear of embarrassment.

Reserving or waiting for a court

There are many different ways of obtaining a public tennis court some of which even confuse the average and advanced player. Some venues have sign-up chalkboards, while others use the hanging of a racket on a board. There's also the honor system.

At clubs and resorts and with some public park systems it is often possible to pre-reserve a court.

If you have claim to a court and your partner has not arrived yet, you may put your racket up against the net to hold the court until your partner arrives.

If there are more players than courts available, it is always nice to propose a doubles game. This shows courtesy and could also be a way to make more tennis friends.

Walking onto the Court

Try not to distract players who are already on the court by entering gates or walking behind players who are actively playing a game. Wait until the point is over, and stay close to the fence, before crossing over. It is alright to walk by when people are warming up, but be sure to stop first before walking behind players.

Retrieving balls that have gone into an adjacent court

Unavoidably, sometimes your ball will go into someone else's court.
Be polite and wait until a point is over before asking people in the neighboring court for your ball. Do say you're sorry that your ball has gone into their court.

When a ball from another court has gone into your court, roll the ball back to them when they are ready to receive it. If that ball distracted anyone on your court, be sure to play a "let", i.e. play the point over.

Never enter into another court to retrieve your ball, unless you are sure you are not disturbing the players in that court.

Avoid Noise

Respect others by not making a lot of noise, yelling, etc. Better to leave the portable stereo (boom box) at home.

Your opponent shouting or talking

When your opponent shouts in disgust when his shot is terrible or too short and this disturbs your play, you automatically (are supposed to) receive the point. Its best to give a polite warning: If this happens again you lose the point.

If your opponent constantly makes conversation after each point, and this disturbs your concentration, tell them in a nice way you want to talk less so you can better concentrate.

Never talk to a player on another court who is actively playing a point. Wait till he is done, or when you return a ball to him.

Other Disturbances

If there's a tremendous disturbance near your court, can you ask for a "let"? The rules say you can only ask for a let if the disturbance is in front of you. An airplane flying overhead, a baby starting to cry or a dog barking, are no reasons to receive a let.

Not sure about the call

If you are not sure whether a ball hit by your opponent is in or out, can you ask to play the point over? Following recreational tennis etiquette, most players will call the ball good when they are unsure. If the opponent has seen their ball go out, they will correct your call, and call it out.

Who should furnish the tennis balls?

Alternate with your partner if you play on a regular basis.

Walking by a court where a match is going on

When a match is going on avoid getting in view of players on that court. Stay back. Don't walk close to their fence.

Don't be a Court Hog

Players who occupy their court for over an hour while others are waiting, are court hogs. You cannot justify holding your court for more than an hour.

Be polite and considerate, but stand your ground

Think very positive while on the tennis court, but be ready to defend yourself in a polite but fair way. Be courteous and considerate and establish a reputation for being a good person on the tennis court. Have mutual respect. Don't try to win "at all costs". In most cases you will be required to keep your own score, call your own lines, and even calling lines against yourself if you see it better than your opponent.

We know there are people who call unfair lines, and they usually get a reputation for such behavior.

Remember it is nice to give a compliment to your opponent—"Good shot".

Always be on time. Respect your self and your opponent. Control your emotions, even in adverse circumstances.
Sportsmanship is an internalized attitude that reflects itself on and off the court. Good sports have a healthy attitude about playing in competition.

Also, it is appropriate to shake hands after the match, win or lose. When we talk about sportsmanship, we tend to think about on-court behavior, but a person must be gracious after the match as well. Be a good sport.

Choosing a Tennis Racket

There is such a variety of rackets to choose from nowadays, how do you ever know which one is right for you? It's not easy. On the other hand, there are so many options that it's definitely possible to find a racket that will be right for you, and improve your game.

Over the years, rackets loose their power. So, depending on how often and how hard you play, it makes sense to shop for rackets every 3-5 years, or more often if your re-stinger says your racket is wearing out.

Selecting a racket involves both practical and emotional considerations.

First the practical considerations:

The best thing is to try a number of different rackets. Get a demo from your dealer or Pro and hit with it, before you decide which one to buy.
Most rackets are made of a composite material, including fiberglass, graphite, magnesium, boron, aluminum, molded epoxy, etc.

A good composite racket costs close to $100 and up, with some of the most advanced models going for well over $200. Be prepared to spend at least about $100 and then let your "hands-on" experience guide you.

It's impossible to generalize about the "feel" of composite rackets. Most offer more power than previous models, and in recent years racket frames have become lighter and lighter.

Some rackets are stiffer, others are more flexible. Generally, stiffer racket frames give more power, while flexible rackets give more control and feel of the ball. Some rackets have built-in shock absorbance, which is especially attractive for those who are prone to tennis elbow.

No matter what your racket is made of, it must feel comfortable. This depends on its weight, balance and grip size.

Racket frames, today, range in weight from 8-13 ounces. Highly experienced players tend to play with medium-heavy rackets. Most recreational players play with relatively light frames. Heavier rackets better absorb the vibrations, caused by the impact of the ball on the strings, and are easier on the arm and elbow than extremely light rackets.

A racket should feel comfortable right away, but beware of choosing a racket just because it is light. If you choose one that is too light, you may end up putting too much wrist action in your shots. Ideally, the racket must feel like a natural extension of the arm and shoulder, and be easy to swing.

Adult tennis rackets used to all be 27 inches long, but now rackets are offered in 27-28.5 inch length. Added length adds power and reach, at the expense of control. Some people prefer the longer rackets because it improves their serve.

Rackets vary in head size, from a compact 85 square inches to oversized rackets up to 135 square inches. As racket head size increases, the "sweet spot" gets larger, and it becomes easier to hit with power. However, with a larger head size, you lose maneuverability, especially at the net, so most players choose rackets in the 95-110 square inches head size.

Balance refers to how the weight is distributed in the racket frame. Rackets of equal weight may feel quite different because of the way their weight is distributed. Some rackets feel heavier, because more of its weight is in the head, while others feel quite light because their weight is more concentrated in the handle.

To test for balance in an unstrung racket, find the middle of the racket and rest it on a straight edge. To compensate for the strings, place a ½ ounce weight on the racket head. If the racket remains level, it is evenly balanced. If it tilts, it is either "head heavy" or "head light".

A "head light" racket is often preferred by players who spend a lot of time at the net, like doubles players. A head light racket can boost players' speed in reacting to volley opportunities at the net.

Head-heavy rackets have their weight more concentrated in the racket head. This puts additional mass behind ground strokes, so these tend to be favored by heavy hitters.

The grip size is determined by the circumference of the handle. The most common sizes are (in inches) 41/8, 41/4, 43/8, 41/2, 45/8 and 43/4.

To find your correct size, measure the distance from the long crease in the middle of your palm to the tip of your ring finger.

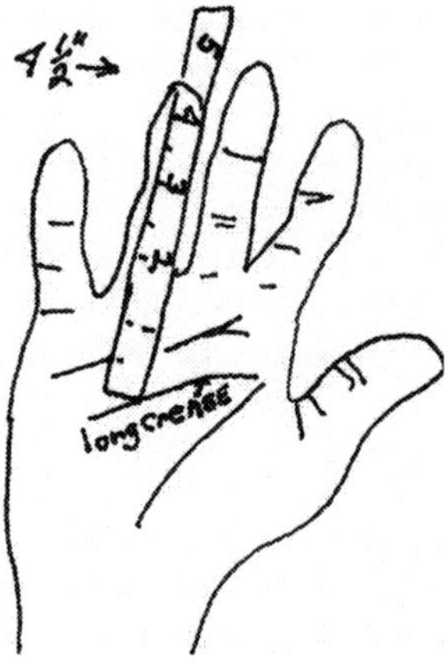

More likely than not, you will find this distance to be one of the lengths listed above. This is the first grip size you should try. But don't go by the ruler alone. Always test the grip to make certain that it feels good in your hand.

Beyond practical considerations, there are emotional considerations for choosing a racket, and you might as well recognize them. Some people may think responding to our emotions is silly, but, believe it or not, much of what we buy is influenced by emotional as well as rational considerations.

The whole idea of wanting to get a new racket could be because you feel you deserve something new. It feels good to get new shoes, a new car, so why not a new racket?

Some people favor a certain brand of racket, because they have had success with that brand before. Unfortunately, all brands keep changing their rackets specs, and sometimes it is impossible to replace the racket that you are giving up.

Or you may feel inclined to try a brand just because it is very popular, or because there is a tennis pro or other player you admire, who plays with that brand. This may be a purely an emotional thing.

If you feel favorable towards a brand, for whatever reason, by all means do look among that brand's rackets to see if there is one you really like the feel of.

Beyond brand, you may be influenced by the looks of the racket. If you have the choice between two rackets that feel equally good, buy the one that looks the best to you. If it makes you look good, you'll feel good, and play better.

Re-stringing and Choosing String

You might wait till you break a string, but, actually, your string loses its resiliency over time, and you should consider re-stringing your racket regularly.

The general rule about re-stringing your racket is that you do it as often per year as you play per week. In other words, if you play, on average, twice a week, you should have your racket re-strung every 6 months. Of course, if you break your strings more often than that, you replace them more often. But if that's the case, you might want to try to find a more durable string.

In selecting strings, you can buy several types of upgrades from the cheapest nylon.

- More "durability"—especially desirable if you keep breaking your strings often
- More "performance", like power, feel or "touch"; this can be an issue for advanced players
- Special function string, for example, allowing for more "spin", or creating less vibration

Most of this can be addressed by the thickness of the string you select. String comes in different gauges. Gauge 15 is the thickest, and generally most durable string. Thinner strings (17 and 18 gauge) provide more feel, impart spin better, and are usually less durable. Gauge 16 presents a nice compromise.

There is a staggering variation in materials used in string, and unless you are hyper-involved in tennis, it is no use trying to learn the characteristics of each. Just ask your stringer to use a quality "synthetic gut" in the thickness you prefer.

Aside from the thickness of the string, you will have to decide on string tension. Your racket frame will have a range, for example from 50-60 pounds, or from 55-65 pounds. You decide whether you want the stringing to be in the upper, middle or lower end of this range. When you select the string tension to be in then upper range for your frame, you tend to get more control. When you select the string tension to be at the lower end of the range, you get more power, because the ball will "trampoline" more. This usually goes at the expense of control.

Most important of all: Make sure your string and racket do not over-heat. String, and the frame itself, can deteriorate rapidly if heated above 110 degrees Fahrenheit. Never leave a racket in a locked car. Temperatures can easily reach 140 degrees in a closed car, and this will ruin your strings. Also, avoid extreme cold, so take your racket on-board when traveling by plane. A racket does not belong in the unheated cargo space of an airplane.

Tennis Elbow

Tennis elbow is a painful inflammation of the muscles that extend (and straighten) the wrist and forearm. It is really an injury of the forearm, but the pain is most intense in the small area where the tendons attach to the elbow, called the epicondyle.

The outer epicondyle is involved in almost all cases, although the inner epicondyle may sometimes be affected as well. The pain is caused by swelling of the tissues of the epicondyle.

How to tell if you have it: Hold your arm out horizontally, bent at the elbow and make a fist. Have a friend grasp your fist with one hand to stabilize your arm. Then have him squeeze your elbow with the other hand. If you feel pain in the elbow joint, you have tennis elbow.

The most likely group to suffer from tennis elbow are middle aged players of average to above average ability who play 2-3 times per week. Tennis elbow is uncommon among beginners and infrequent recreational players.

In the middle years (35-50), the body's strength and flexibility begin to decline. However, the enthusiasm of youth has not been tempered by the same degree. Players overdo it; overuse their arms, which puts stresses on tissues that are loosing their resiliency.

Muscular imbalance, lack of flexibility and poor endurance may lead to tennis elbow. The repetitive nature of tennis strokes can be a definite contributing factor to the pain of tennis elbow.

Oftentimes tennis elbow can be linked to a technically faulty backhand stroke. If you suspect this, by all means check with a tennis instructor to have your stroke analyzed.

The backhand must be hit with the full arm, from the shoulder. The moment of contact with the ball must be "out in front", not beside the body. If the player uses the forearm and elbow, rather than the full arm, in the backhand, tennis elbow is a likely result.

The best way to reduce the immediate pain of tennis elbow is to give your arm a rest. Rest and ice may used to ease the pain. You may want to use a medication that reduces inflammation. If pain persists, consult a doctor who can prescribe a strong anti-inflammatory drug.

How to Play a Tie-Breaker

12 Point Tie-breaker

If announced or agreed upon in advance, a tie-breaker game is used when the score reaches 6-6 in any set.

The player (or doubles team) that wins seven points wins the game and the set, provided he or she leads by two points. Otherwise the tie-breaker game is continued until one player leads by 2 points. Numerical scoring is used throughout the tie-breaker (1,2,3 etc.)

In singles, the person's who's turn it is to serve is the server for the first point, from the right side of the court (The "deuce" side). Next, the opponent is the server for the second and third point. He or she serves first from the left side of the court (the "add" side) and then from the right or deuce side. Thereafter, each player serves for two consecutive points, always first from the left side, then the right side, until there is a winner.

During a tie-breaker game, players change ends after each six points, without resting. At the conclusion of the tie-breaker, players or doubles teams change ends again. The player or team that served first in the tie-breaker, receives first in the next set.

9-Point Tie-breaker

The nine point tie-breaker is sometimes used in sets played with the "No Ad" scoring system. (This system may be used in a variety of tournaments to speed up play. As the name suggests, whoever gets the first point after "deuce" wins the game).

In singles, the player whose turn it is to serve is the server for the first and second point, starting on the right side, then the left side. The opponent serves the next two serves, again starting on the right side, then the left side.

Players change ends after four points If the score reaches four all, the second server gets to serve the final point. His opponent has the option to choose whether the serve is hit from the left or the right side.

When playing doubles, each player serves two serves from the same end of the court that he or she served from during the set.

The players stay on the same ends for one game of the next set, with the team that served second in the tiebreaker now serving first.

Ways to Set Up Recreational Tournaments

There a number of different ways in which you can set up recreational tennis tournaments. In recreational tennis, the general principle is to allow for the maximum number of matches for all that enter the tournament.

The following factors need to be considered to organize a successful tournament:

- Number of entries
- Length of the tournament (sessions or time frame)
- Facilities available

Tournaments can follow a number of different formats which are described below.

The Round-Robin Format.

One of the most popular tournaments is the Round Robin, because you can get maximum participation by members. There is a basic formula which enables the director-organizer of a round robin tournament to arrange for the maximum number of matches:

Formula: N(N-1)/2 where N is the umber of entries.

If there are 16 entries, the total number of matches is 16(16-1)/2= 120 games

So, with 16 entries, 120 games or matches will be played total, based on 15 rounds of 8 matches.

Making the draw is easy. Each team or entry is given a number and placed for the first round of play. After the first round, all teams or entries rotate one position clockwise except for team one which stays put. The following example is for a round robin tournament with 10 participants:

ROUND ROBIN TOURNAMENT MATCH DRAW with 10 Participants:

				Round:				
I	II	III	IV	V	VI	VII	VIII	IX
1-10	1-2	1-3	1-4	1-5	1-6	1-7	1-8	1-9
2-9	3-10	4-2	5-3	6-4	7-5	8-6	9-7	10-8
3-8	4-9	5-10	6-2	7-3	8-4	9-5	10-6	2-7
4-7	5-8	6-9	7-10	8-2	9-3	10-4	2-5	3-6
5-6	6-7	7-8	8-9	9-10	10-2	2-3	3-4	4-5

If there are an uneven number of entries, they symbol BYE is used. This means the team matched with a BYE has no opponent for that particular round.

Example: 3 teams with one BYE:

	Round	
I	II	III
1-BYE	1-2	1-3
2-3	3-BYE	BYE-2

The Ladder Tournament

The Ladder tournament is a very good format for tennis. It requires very little supervision. Players can arrange their own times and matches.

Coaches like to set up ladders when there are large numbers of players competing for positions on the team, both varsity and junior varsity.

The name of each player in the tournament is placed on a card or tag (Tong depressors work well too). A display is made where the name cards are put in order. With 8 players is looks like this:

Name 8
Name 7
Name 6
Name 5
Name 4
Name 3
Name 2
Name 1

Players may challenge players one or two rungs above their own name for a match. If the challenger wins, the positions of the two names are exchanged on the ladder. Usually, the rule is that if a challenger loses, he or she must accept another challenge before being able to re-challenge the original opponent.

The Pyramid Tournament

The pyramid tournament is an adaptation of the Ladder format. It is especially suitable for a larger number of entries.

The names of all players are placed on tags and arranged in a pyramid rather than a ladder:

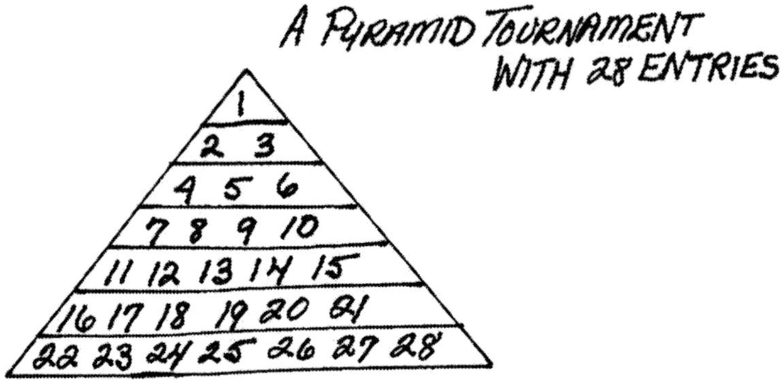

In this type of tournament a player may challenge anyone in the row directly above them, or anyone on their left in the same row.

If the higher ranked player loses, he exchanges his place with the challenger.

The overall winner is the person who is at the top of the pyramid at the end of the tournament. Most pyramids also award a prize to the winner of each row which provides an incentive for the less skilled players as well.

Single Elimination Tournament

There are basically three types of elimination tournaments. They are limited in range and thus more economical in terms of time and facilities required, certainly compared to a round robin tournament.

Elimination tournaments can be based on 4, 8, 16, 32 and 64 entries. If there are, for example, only 12 entries, you use the 16 entry draw format with the addition of 4 BYEs.

In a single elimination tournament a single defeat eliminates the entry from the tournament. Entries are placed and usually drawn with byes equally distributed into top and bottom brackets.

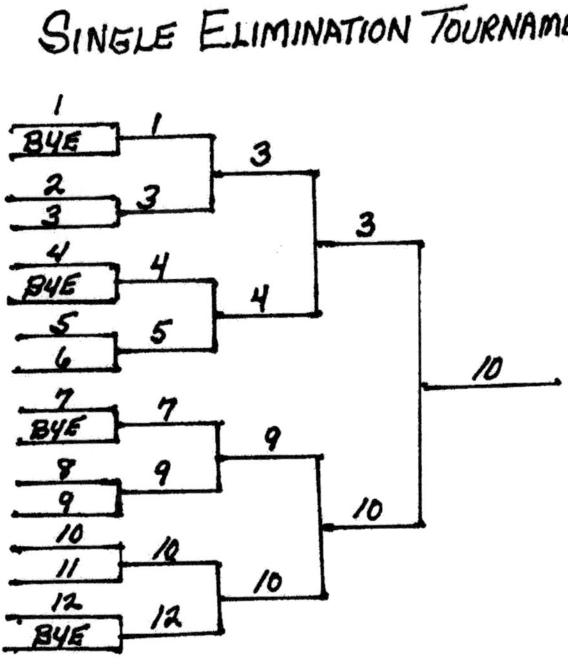

In most cases it is desirable to use seeding, in order to enhance the chances that the best players meet in the finals, and to avoid the chance that the best players meet in an early round.

Common rules for the number of seeds:

Number of seeds:	No fewer than....entries
2	8
4	16
6	24
8	32
12	48
16	64

Placement of seeds:

2 seeds:	#1 at the top half of the draw, #2 at the bottom of the bottom half
4 seeds:	#1 and #2 as above; #3 and #4, drawn by lot. First drawn is placed at the bottom of the third quarter and the second drawn at the top of the second quarter
6 seeds:	#1-#4 as above. #5 and #6 drawn by lot. First drawn is placed at the bottom of the seventh-eighth and the second drawn at the top of the second-eighth

Double Elimination

In this type of tournament a team or player must lose two games before it is eliminated. The formula for the number of games to be played is 2(N-1)+1.

The final game will match a team which has won all its games against a team with only one loss. In case the team that has lost one game defeats the unbeaten team, the outcome is a tie, since now both teams have lost once. This leads to the play-off match between the same team (the +1 in the formula).

The draw looks rather complicated. Note that the boxed teams lost in the first round, and move to the left, winners move over to the right. Each team that loses for the second time is eliminated, a team that loses in later rounds on the right, moves over to play a winner on the left side of the draw.

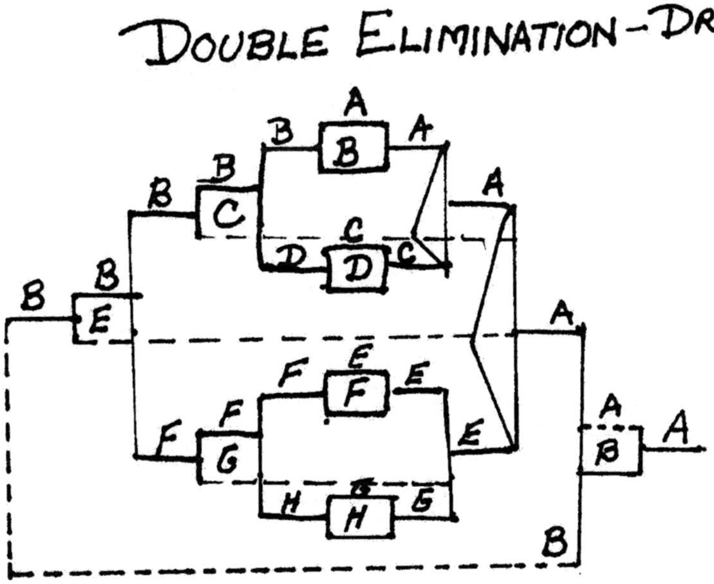

Elimination Consolation

An elimination consolation tournament is a compromise between single and double elimination. It guarantees that each team or player will play at least two matches.

First round winners move to the right, first round losers move to the left, so that a winners and a consolation bracket is formed.

The champion and runner up come from the winners bracket. The winner of the consolation bracket does not play winner of the winners bracket.

Here is an example of a 7 team Elimination-Consolation draw. Note how team #1, having a BYE in the first round, but losers in their first match, still moves to the consolation bracket for a second match.

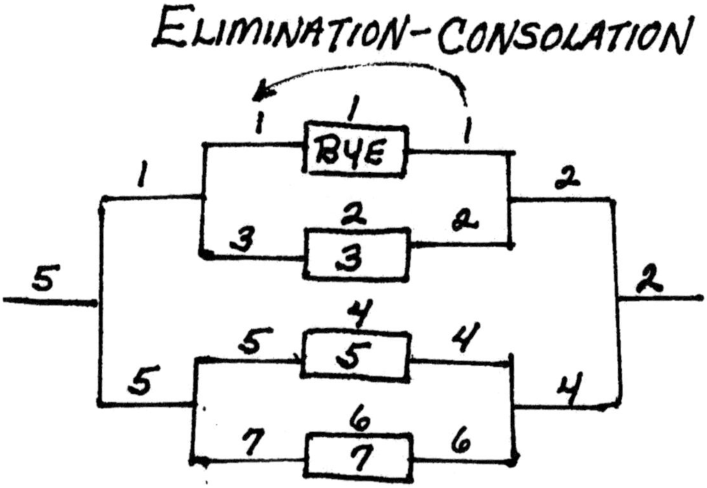

13

Personal Stories

When the Garfield Tennis Courts were Clay (Ron's Story)

I spent most of my young adult years chasing a dream to become an outstanding tennis player. To transform your dreams into reality means you must take charge of your attitude and turn it into action.

Most of my playing days were spent on the Garfield Park tennis courts in Indianapolis. Tennis was a dream and adventure for me as I formulated an above average tennis game with the fundamentals I learned form the older gentlemen who played at the courts. I had no formal lessons.

I began to be known as a product of Garfield. I took pride in my meager tennis equipment as I followed a dream to two junior championships. The time of getting out of school #34 and running home to get to the park was coming to an end.

I thought I was headed for Indiana University but they gave their last scholarship to the Chicago Junior Champion. My high school never had a tennis team.

Then my father lost his job, I graduated from high school and broke my racket all in a two-week period. A heart-breaking situation indeed. We moved to Lansing Michigan, the home of Michigan State University and the Spartans.

At the time I was racketless, and in the days that followed I felt bitter every time I thought that I was headed towards failure.

Fortunately, my grades in high school were exceptional and I graduated in the top ten of my class. So one of my first instincts was to visit Michigan state and try to get into the school.
Finally I made a connection to get a try out with the tennis coach, but I do not think I was taken very seriously.

With only three dollars in my pocket I was faced with a bigger problem: Where was I going to get a good racket and strings. I walked around East Lansing for several hours. The crisis seemed to be getting larger and larger. I was in search of an idea, and had to make a decision fast. Finally I came upon a hobby shop-sports shop…

In my early years as a youngster I had started to collect stamps, and for several years my relatives had mailed me stamps, new and used stamps. I took my modest stamp collection to the hobby shop as a down payment on a tennis racket and some new string.

Later that week I impressed the Michigan state coach, and received a partial academic athletic scholarship with the opportunity to work in the athletic work program.

In 1960, I won a Big Ten Tennis Championship at No. 5 singles. In my first year on the varsity, I defeated the Chicago Jr. Champion, the one who had gotten the last scholarship to Indian, in three sets. As my (basketball) high school coach always used to say: "To be a champion you must sometimes suffer a heartbreak"

How I Found Out About Yoga (Chris' story)

During the Summer of 2000, I had a totally unexpected injury. Seemingly "out of the blue", I contracted a staph infection in my left hip. It took an emergency operation and several months of recovery to get back on my feet and walk again. At that point I felt "ready" to go back to one of my passions, tennis. However, to my shock and horror, my doctor told me I couldn't jump or have any impact on the hip for another year! Wow, that was a setback.

In one of the places where I play tennis, the SPAC athletic center at Northwestern University, I knew there was some kind of stretching class going on at the same early morning hour that I was often there to play tennis. It seemed like a very pleasant peaceful type of session, with nice classical music played on the side. So, for lack of being able to play tennis, I decided to check out what this class was all about, and it turned out to be a yoga class.

I did not have an altogether positive image of yoga. I always imagined it to be difficult, for extremely flexible people who put themselves in all kinds of impossible, pretzel-like contortions.

But since I was there, I decided to give it a try, and I still remember what a revelation it was to me, that very first yoga class, even if I could only do about half of what everyone else there did. I felt rather embarrassed, especially because there were (including myself) only three guys and more than a dozen women in the session. But afterwards, I felt fantastic, light, almost like I was floating. I came back, and back, and after about four sessions I was hooked. Whenever possible, I now attend two yoga classes a week.

I have also started doing yoga on my own, several times a week. I have discovered it is easy to do in hotel rooms when I am traveling for work, and so much more rewarding than using the cramped workout rooms you find in most hotels.

When the time came for my check-up, my doctor was amazed about the range of motion I had in my hip. The X-ray showed that the cartilage had grown back, so I was cleared for tennis again, three months earlier than expected.

Now that I am back to tennis, I find I am better able to concentrate and control my game. I am more patient, and am more able to focus on the game, one shot at a time. I have much more control over my emotions, and am able to use breathing as a way to focus my concentration and relax between points. All in all, I am playing at a higher level than before my injury.

Also, yoga teaches you how your body is put together, and which muscle groups are intended for what type of activity. For example, you learn to lengthen the spine and to balance your head better on your neck and shoulders. Another great lesson is how your arms connect to your shoulder blades. This is a great help in visualizing how to use the entire arm, from the shoulder on down, when you're hitting ground strokes.

Yoga has become a long-term discovery process for me. Just as in tennis, there are so many different things to learn, so many things that you gradually get better at over time.

Best of all, it starts to affect almost everything about you. You start to like how you feel, how you stand, how you move, how you breathe, how you think about your relationships with others. It enhances your energy level, stimulates your digestion and even regulates your bowel movements. Give yoga a try.

To order more copies of this book, contact www.iuniverse.com

To order by mail, contact

Ron Mescall
2755 Van Buren Avenue
Dubuque, Iowa 52001

Please include $2.50 for shipping and handling and $0.90 for Iowa sales tax.

0-595-32333-2

CPSIA information can be obtained at www.ICGtesting.com
Printed in the USA
LVOW06s0022091015

457593LV00001B/26/P

9 780595 323333